# Biography Today

*Profiles
of People
of Interest
to Young
Readers*

Volume 15
Issue 1
January 2006

**Cherie D. Abbey**
*Managing Editor*

**Kevin Hillstrom**
*Editor*

*Omnigraphics*

*615 Griswold Str*
*Detroit, Michigan*

D1468244

**Omnigraphics, Inc.**

Cherie D. Abbey, *Managing Editor*
Kevin Hillstrom, *Editor*

Laurie Hillstrom, *Sketch Writer*

Allison A. Beckett, Mary Butler, and Linda Strand, *Research Staff*

\* \* \*

Peter E. Ruffner, *Publisher*
Frederick G. Ruffner, Jr., *Chairman*
Matthew P. Barbour, *Senior Vice President*
Kay Gill, *Vice President—Directories*

\* \* \*

Elizabeth Barbour, *Research and Permissions Coordinator*
David P. Bianco, *Marketing Director*
Leif A. Gruenberg, *Development Manager*
Kevin Hayes, *Operations Manager*
Barry Puckett, *Librarian*
Cherry Stockdale, *Permissions Assistant*

Shirley Amore, Kevin Glover, Martha Johns,
Kirk Kauffman, and Angelesia Thorington, *Administrative Staff*

Copyright © 2006 Omnigraphics, Inc.
ISSN 1058-2347 • ISBN 0-7808-0812-6

The information in this publication was compiled from the sources cited and from other sources considered reliable. While every possible effort has been made to ensure reliability, the publisher will not assume liability for damages caused by inaccuracies in the data, and makes no warranty, express or implied, on the accuracy of the information contained herein.

This book is printed on acid-free paper meeting the ANSI Z39.48 Standard. The infinity symbol that appears above indicates that the paper in this book meets that standard.

Printed in the United States

INDEXED IN
Children's Magazine Guide

# Contents

# Preface

*Biography Today* is a magazine designed and written for the young reader—ages 9 and above—and covers individuals that librarians and teachers tell us that young people want to know about most: entertainers, athletes, writers, illustrators, cartoonists, and political leaders.

## The Plan of the Work

The publication was especially created to appeal to young readers in a format they can enjoy reading and readily understand. Each issue contains approximately 10 sketches arranged alphabetically. Each entry provides at least one picture of the individual profiled, and bold-faced rubrics lead the reader to information on birth, youth, early memories, education, first jobs, marriage and family, career highlights, memorable experiences, hobbies, and honors and awards. Each of the entries ends with a list of easily accessible sources designed to lead the student to further reading on the individual and a current address. Retrospective entries are also included, written to provide a perspective on the individual's entire career.

Biographies are prepared by Omnigraphics editors after extensive research, utilizing the most current materials available. Those sources that are generally available to students appear in the list of further reading at the end of the sketch.

## Indexes

Cumulative indexes are an important component of *Biography Today*. Each issue of the *Biography Today* General Series includes a Cumulative Names Index, which comprises all individuals profiled in *Biography Today* since the series began in 1992. In addition, we compile three other indexes: the Cumulative General Index, Places of Birth Index, and Birthday Index. See our web site, www.biographytoday.com, for these three indexes, along with the Names Index. All *Biography Today* indexes are cumulative, including all individuals profiled in both the General Series and the Subject Series.

# Our Advisors

This series was reviewed by an Advisory Board comprised of librarians, children's literature specialists, and reading instructors to ensure that the concept of this publication—to provide a readable and accessible biographical magazine for young readers—was on target. They evaluated the title as it developed, and their suggestions have proved invaluable. Any errors, however, are ours alone. We'd like to list the Advisory Board members, and to thank them for their efforts.

Our Advisory Board stressed to us that we should not shy away from controversial or unconventional people in our profiles, and we have tried to follow their advice. The Advisory Board also mentioned that the sketches might be useful in reluctant reader and adult literacy programs, and we would value any comments librarians might have about the suitability of our magazine for those purposes.

# Your Comments Are Welcome

Our goal is to be accurate and up-to-date, to give young readers information they can learn from and enjoy. Now we want to know what you think. Take a look at this issue of *Biography Today*, on approval. Write or call me with your comments. We want to provide an excellent source of biographical information for young people. Let us know how you think we're doing.

Cherie Abbey
Managing Editor, *Biography Today*
Omnigraphics, Inc.
615 Griswold Street
Detroit, MI 48226

editor@biographytoday.com
www.biographytoday.com

# Congratulations!

Congratulations to the following individuals and libraries, who are receiving a free copy of *Biography Today*, Vol. 15, No. 1, for suggesting people who appear in this issue:

Patricia Earl, Romeo High School Library, Romeo, MI

Lucille M. Koors, Manual High School Media Center,
    Indianapolis, IN

Shatonna Lucius, Chicago, IL

Howard Norris, Toledo, OH

Stephanie Nunez, North Heights, CA

Steven Ott, Oak Lawn, IL

Marissa Rayford, Riverdale, MD

Tiffany Wood, Lehigh Acres, FL

## Carol Bellamy 1942-

American Lawyer, Politician, and Social Activist
Served as Executive Director of UNICEF and
Director of the Peace Corps

### BIRTH

Carol Bellamy was born on January 14, 1942, in Plainfield,
New Jersey. She was the oldest of two children born to Lou
Bellamy, a telephone installer, and his wife Frances, a nurse.
She has one younger brother, Robert.

### YOUTH AND EDUCATION

Bellamy grew up in Scotch Plains, New Jersey. She has
described herself as "a pretty independent kid. . . . I never

really discussed things with anybody. I just made up my own mind." As a student at Scotch Plains-Fanwood High School, Bellamy acted in student plays, participated in sports, sang in the choir, and served as president of the debate club.

After graduating from high school around 1960, Bellamy enrolled at Gettysburg College in Pennsylvania, where she studied sociology and psychology. While studying in the college library one night, she came across a pamphlet describing a new service organization called the Peace Corps.

The Peace Corps was established by the U.S. government in 1961. It is a program that sends volunteers (usually college-aged students) to live and work in developing nations, where they support and train local communities in such skills as farming, technology, health, business practices, construction, and environmental preservation. Bellamy was inspired to join the Peace Corps after earning her bachelor's degree in 1963. "I was a bright-eyed, bushy-tailed liberal-arts graduate ready to save the world," she said of her decision. "I was absolutely unqualified to do anything."

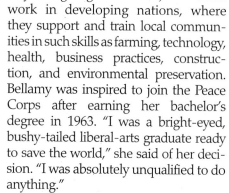

*Bellamy was inspired to join the Peace Corps after finishing college. "I was a bright-eyed, bushy-tailed liberal-arts graduate ready to save the world," she said of her decision. "I was absolutely unqualified to do anything."*

Bellamy served for two years in the Central American nation of Guatemala. During this time, she worked on a chicken farm, ran a lunch program for schoolchildren, and hosted a radio show called "The Housewife's Hour" that promoted family health and nutrition. Bellamy learned a great deal from her experiences in the Peace Corps. "What I took out of the Peace Corps was that you need to be willing to try a lot of different things, and actually fail in some things," she related. "You get up and wipe your nose, and head forward." She also said that spending two years in Guatemala showed her that "there's a whole big world out there and you ought to give it a try."

Bellamy's time in the Peace Corps raised her interest in politics and international relations. Upon returning to the United States in 1965, she enrolled in the School of Law at New York University. She worked as a waitress in order to pay for her tuition and expenses, and she earned her law degree in 1968.

## CAREER HIGHLIGHTS

Armed with her Peace Corps experience and law degree, Bellamy accepted a job as an associate attorney in a prestigious New York law firm in 1968. In addition to her work with the firm, she used her legal skills to help people in several other ways. For example, at that time organized demonstrations to oppose the Vietnam War were common, and many protesters were arrested. Bellamy helped create a group called the Lawyers Committee to End the War, which provided pro bono (free) legal services to people who were arrested for protesting against the war. She also joined the Council of New York Law Associates, which enabled her to support community organizations and antipoverty programs while learning about public policy issues. This experience provided her with a good foundation to enter politics.

### Entering Public Service and Politics

Bellamy served for one year as the assistant commissioner for New York City's Department of Mental Health. Then, in 1972, she decided to run for the New York State Senate. She was elected and served two terms in office. One of the issues she supported during her campaign was passage of the Equal Rights Amendment (ERA), which would have changed the U.S. Constitution to specifically ensure legal equality between men and women. Although the New York State legislature voted to ratify (approve) the amendment, it was eventually defeated when it failed to be ratified by two-thirds of the states.

At the end of her second term as a state senator, Bellamy considered running for several higher offices, including the U.S. Congress and the New York State attorney general. She eventually set her sights on becoming the president of the New York City Council. As head of the group that works with the mayor and other officials to run the city's affairs, the council president is the second-most-powerful job in city government. Bellamy won the Democratic Party primary (a preliminary election to determine the final slate of candidates who compete in the general election). She beat four men, including the sitting council president, Paul O'Dwyer. In the general election she earned over 80 percent of the vote to beat her Republican opponent, John A. Esposito. Elected in 1978, Bellamy became the first female president of the New York City Council.

The liberal-minded Bellamy quickly gained notice for her outspokenness and activism. She made headlines because of her frequent clashes with the city's mayor, Ed Koch, on such issues as public safety, social services, taxes, and budgets. In her seven years in office, Bellamy led notable

*Bellamy in her office in 1981, as president of the New York City Council.*

improvements in the areas of public transportation, mental health services, and gay rights. "If you were a woman in the public arena, you were expected by your constituents to carry an additional burden, to automatically represent women's issues," she recalled of her career in politics. "I could say I'd rather talk about the city's pothole problems, but the reality was that if I didn't bring women's and children's issues up, no one else did."

In 1985 Bellamy decided to run against Koch in hopes of becoming the Democratic Party candidate for mayor of New York City. She was the first woman ever to run for mayor of the nation's largest city. In her campaign, Bellamy emphasized the need to improve the city's social services, infrastructure, housing, and transportation. When Koch defeated her and other opponents in the Democratic primary, Bellamy decided to run in the general election as the candidate of the Liberal Party. Koch won the general election as well, though, gaining almost 80 percent of the vote, while Bellamy earned only 10 percent.

In order to run for mayor, Bellamy had to step down from her position on the city council. When her term ended on January 1, 1986, she accepted a new job as an investment banker with Morgan Stanley & Co. Bellamy's work in finance continued to focus on community issues, such as providing funds for the improvement of schools and hospitals. "If it hadn't been about making people's lives better, I couldn't have done it," she said of her work in investment banking.

After four years out of the public eye, Bellamy decided to run for the office of state comptroller in New York. The comptroller is in charge of overseeing the state's finances and pension fund. The campaign against her Republican opponent, Edward V. Regan, was heated and controversial. Bellamy narrowly lost the election and returned to her work in investment banking, this time with Bear Stearns Companies. In 1993 Regan resigned, and she appealed to state lawmakers to appoint her to the position. As Bellamy saw it, her strong showing in the 1990 election indicated that voters supported her for the job. But the governor of New York, Mario Cuomo, promoted another candidate instead.

## Becoming Director of the Peace Corps

Bellamy's many achievements in law, politics, and finance—as well as her reputation as an activist for liberal causes—caught the attention of President Bill Clinton. (For more information on Clinton, see *Biography Today General Series* July 1992 and Updates in the Annual Cumulations for 1994–2001.) Shortly after taking office in 1993, Clinton offered Bellamy the opportunity to serve in his administration as either deputy secretary of transportation or director of the Peace Corps. She chose the Peace Corps job, becoming the first volunteer ever to go on to run the organization. "I hoped that, at least as I visited volunteers in the field, I could bring kind of a simpatico for both the highs and the lows, the joys and the sorrows, the difficult moments, the lonely moments, and yet the wonderful exhilarating moments that volunteers experience," she stated.

> *Bellamy was the first Peace Corps volunteer ever to go on to run the organization. "I hoped that, at least as I visited volunteers in the field, I could bring kind of a simpatico for both the highs and the lows, the joys and the sorrows, the difficult moments, the lonely moments, and yet the wonderful exhilarating moments that volunteers experience," she stated.*

In the years before Bellamy took over, the Peace Corps had suffered from funding cuts and poor leadership, so she found herself with many challenges to address. Bellamy decided that her priorities would be to increase the number of volunteers that joined the Peace Corps, improve their training, and ensure their safety. She also focused on publicizing the organization's activities more aggressively and finding ways for returning volunteers to continue their service in the United States, by contributing

*In her role as Executive Director of UNICEF, Bellamy visits
a girls' school in Kabul, Afghanistan, in 2003,
after the fall of the Taliban allowed girls to return to school.*

their skills in schools or other social service agencies. Under her leadership, the Peace Corps increased the number of countries it served as well as the number of volunteers in its ranks.

## Assuming Leadership of UNICEF

Bellamy's high-profile role as the head of the Peace Corps, along with her achievements in the areas of children's health and welfare, made her an excellent candidate to assume leadership of UNICEF. The United Nations International Children's Emergency Fund (UNICEF) was created in 1946 to provide food and health care to children in Europe after World War II. (Although the organization later changed its name to United Nations Children's Emergency Fund, it is still referred to as UNICEF.) Within a few years UNICEF expanded its activities to other parts of the world, wherever children's welfare was threatened by poverty and disease.

In 1995 United Nations Chairman Boutros Boutros-Ghali announced that he was seeking a female candidate to fill the position of executive director of UNICEF. (For more information on Boutros Boutros-Ghali, see *Biography Today General Series* Apr. 1993 and Update in the 1998 Annual Cumulation.) After considering several European candidates, Boutros-Ghali selected Bellamy for the job. As was the case when she took over the

Peace Corps, she immediately faced several problems as head of UNICEF, including a financial scandal. Critics of the organization's previous leadership charged that funds had been poorly managed and misused in some areas.

In addition to addressing these concerns, Bellamy focused on five key priorities for the organization: promoting immunization against disease; ensuring the availability of quality schooling for all boys and girls; limiting the spread of HIV/AIDS and reducing its effect on the lives of young people; protecting children from domestic violence and other forms of abuse and exploitation; and creating early childhood programs to ensure that very young children were healthy and ready for school. "I can think of no work that is more vital to humanity than working to ensure that children everywhere survive their early years and grow up with health, dignity, and peace," she said of her role in UNICEF.

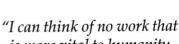

*"I can think of no work that is more vital to humanity than working to ensure that children everywhere survive their early years and grow up with health, dignity, and peace," Bellamy said of her role in UNICEF.*

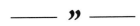

Bellamy encouraged world leaders to realize that investing in the health, education, and safety of children would help end poverty and instability in their countries. She also expanded UNICEF's focus to address the abuse and exploitation of children around the world who are forced to perform dangerous jobs, serve as soldiers, or work as slaves. As part of her job, Bellamy often visited 20 or more countries a year. She went to the war-torn nation of Afghanistan, for instance, to address the Taliban, the strict Islamic government that ruled the country from 1996 until 2001. Bellamy challenged the Taliban to change its policy forbidding girls to attend school. She also met with leaders of African countries where HIV/AIDS affects the lives of millions of children.

In 2002 the United Nations General Assembly on Children held a special session in New York City. This international conference about the issues facing children worldwide was attended by over 7,000 people, including heads of state and other government officials, as well as leaders in the fields of business, academics, and religion. At Bellamy's invitation, hundreds of children from around the world also appeared at the conference to make presentations to the "grown-ups" in attendance. In a speech before the assembled dignitaries, Bellamy asked: "Are you getting all your

*Bellamy speaking to Sri Lankan children forced into a relief camp by the devastating tsunami.*

children into the classroom? Are you protecting all your children against disease? Are they safe from abuse, exploitation, and violence? Unfortunately, we already know the answers. We know we have work to do." The conference resulted in a document titled "A World Fit for Children," which established 21 goals toward promoting the health and welfare of children worldwide. It was adopted by 180 nations.

Another focus of Bellamy's tenure at UNICEF was the importance of meeting the needs of women and mothers in order to build stability for children everywhere. In many countries around the world, women face limited opportunities for education and jobs, physical abuse by husbands and family members, poor health care, and other threats to their well-being. "As women are the primary caretakers of children around the world, the better off women are, the better off their children are," Bellamy explained. "When women are educated, when they are moderately empowered to earn an income, and are generally healthy, their children are more likely to survive, go to school, and grow into productive citizens themselves. That is why educating girls and ensuring the rights of women is central to the vision of UNICEF." Charles MacCormack, president of Save the Children, an international organization dedicated to children's health, praised Bellamy's efforts. "There's no way that children will survive and thrive if their mothers are not healthy and literate," he noted. "Carol was a pioneer in drawing attention to this very crucial reality."

While Bellamy expanded the scope of UNICEF's work, some people expressed concerns that she had lost sight of the organization's original mission: ensuring children's survival by tending to their most basic and immediate health needs. Pointing out that 10.5 million children died each year before reaching the age of five, critics charged that UNICEF could do more good if it returned its focus to countries with high child mortality rates. Yet Bellamy oversaw a number of impressive achievements as head of UNICEF. During her ten years with the organization, child mortality dropped worldwide, incidents of preventable diseases declined, many countries adopted laws protecting and serving children's needs, and the number of children who did not attend school reached an all-time low. In recognition of her accomplishments, *Forbes* magazine named Bellamy as one of the 100 Most Powerful Women in the World in 2004.

## Becoming CEO and President of World Learning

Education has always been a major priority for Bellamy throughout her career. In 2005, after serving two five-year terms as the head of UNICEF, Bellamy resigned to accept a new position as chief executive officer and president of World Learning. World Learning is a private organization based in Vermont that provides education, training, and other programs to promote understanding, social justice, and economic development among nations and cultures. One of World Learning's programs sends high-school students to live in other countries to study new languages, cultures, and environments. "It's great to follow on from my years at UNICEF, during which I saw very clearly how important education is for both individuals and nations," Bellamy explained. Also in 2005, Bellamy was appointed to the New York State Board of Regents, a panel that sets education policy statewide.

## HOME AND FAMILY

Bellamy, who describes herself as a "workaholic," is unmarried and has no children.

## HOBBIES AND OTHER INTERESTS

Bellamy is a fan of baseball's New York Mets. She also enjoys gardening and hiking. In 1986 she went on an all-women hiking trek through the Himalayas, a mountain range in Tibet.

## HONORS AND AWARDS

Award for Innovation in Public Health (*Discover* magazine): 2004

## FURTHER READING

### Books

*Encyclopedia of World Biography Supplement*, Vol. 25, 2005
*Newsmakers*, 2001

### Periodicals

*Boston Globe*, Dec. 9, 2004
*Chicago Tribune*, Mar. 27, 1994, p.4
*Christian Science Monitor*, Nov. 30, 1983, p.3; Nov. 29, 1995, p.13;
    Dec. 24, 1996, p.12; Apr. 29, 2005, p.7
*Current Biography Yearbook*, 1999
*Los Angeles Times*, Apr. 30, 1995, p.M3
*New York Times*, Oct. 3, 1990, p.B1; Apr. 22, 2002, p.A25; Jan. 14, 2005,
    p.B2
*People*, Nov. 27, 2000, p.203
*Philadelphia Inquirer*, May 25, 1995, p.G8
*Washington Post*, Sep. 29, 1993, p.A21; Mar. 2, 1994, p.B1

### Online Articles

http://ourworld.worldlearning.org
    (*OurWorld*, "UNICEF Director Tapped as New President of World
    Learning," Jan. 18, 2005)
http://www.unicef.org/specialsession
    (UNICEF, "World Leaders Say Yes for Children," May 2005)

### Online Databases

*Biography Resource Center Online*, 2005, articles from *Biography
    Resource Center*, 2001; *Encyclopedia of World Biography Supplement*,
    2005; and *Newsmakers*, 2001

## ADDRESS

Carol Bellamy
World Learning
P.O. Box 676
Kipling Road
Brattleboro, VT 05302-0676

## WORLD WIDE WEB SITES

http://www.peacecorps.gov
http://www.unicef.org
http://www.worldlearning.org

## Miri Ben-Ari 1972?-
Israeli-Born American Violinist and Composer
Known as the Hip-Hop Violinist

### BIRTH

Miri Ben-Ari was born around 1972 (some sources say 1978) in Ramat-Gan, Israel, a middle-class suburb of Tel Aviv. Her father was a violinist. She has described her Jewish family as "culturally aware" but not religious.

### YOUTH

Ben-Ari, known today as the "hip-hop violinist," never heard hip-hop music as a child in Israel. "I grew up in a classical bubble," she laughed. "We never had any other type of music in our home—at least not any type with words." She began taking classical violin lessons when she was six years old. "It was very difficult," she remembered, "and that's why I liked it."

Although Ben-Ari quickly demonstrated great promise as a musician, her violin lessons soon became too expensive for her family. Fortunately, she came to the attention of renowned violinist Isaac Stern, who took a special interest in helping promising young artists. (For more information on Stern, see *Biography Today Performing Artists*, Vol. 1.) Recognizing her gift, Stern gave the young musician a violin of her own and arranged for her to receive a scholarship from the America-Israel Cultural Foundation so that she could continue her lessons. Ben-Ari also took private lessons from Stern and from famed violinist Yehudi Menuhin. Despite her training, however, Ben-Ari felt little connection to classical music. "Growing up, I was always looking for something else, but never heard it," she explained.

> "I grew up in a classical bubble," Ben-Ari laughed. "We never had any other type of music in our home—at least not any type with words."

At the age of 18, Ben-Ari started her mandatory military service (Israel requires all of its citizens to serve two years in the Israeli army). "It directly influenced me and put my life in perspective," she recalled of the experience. "When you go to basic training, every soldier is a soldier. They treat us the same. And I love that because I seriously believe that every individual is just as good as another individual. Nobody's better than anybody else."

During this time, Ben-Ari auditioned for and was chosen to play in the highly selective Israeli Army String Quartet. She felt grateful for this opportunity to continue her musical training. "If you have a bad audition, you might have to say goodbye to your instrument for two years," she noted. "But I had a good audition." Ben-Ari also served during the 1991 Persian Gulf War. Although she never saw combat, she did see Iraqi missiles sailing through the air above Tel Aviv.

It was also during her military stint that Ben-Ari began to branch out from classical music. The first time she heard an album by the acclaimed jazz saxophonist Charlie Parker, she was hooked. "That was the beginning and end. My soul was sold. He's a genius—the way he plays, he's talking to you," she explained. "I just loved it. It's all coming out of love. When you love something, you'll do anything to pursue, develop, evolve, and go with it."

## EDUCATION

Ben-Ari received her early education in Tel Aviv. After completing her military service, she moved from Israel to New York City to study jazz at the Mannes School of Music, and she also continued taking private violin lessons. Further musical education came from the clubs where she performed and the studios where she worked as a background musician. "For the most part I learn on stage and from listening to records, which is real school," she said. "Every time I listen to music I learn. I never stop playing and I will always learn."

## CAREER HIGHLIGHTS

Miri Ben-Ari has brought a new sound to the music world through her crisp, percussive violin and keen ear for melody. From classical to jazz to hip-hop—with forays into pop, blues, Latin, Middle Eastern, klezmer, and Celtic—Ben-Ari has explored multiple musical forms with her violin. Rather than moving progressively through the genres, abandoning one when she picks up another, she has incorporated elements from each into her music. "Music is music," she said simply. "You're always developing, just taking a journey of music. You don't leave one thing. You move on, but you don't leave things behind. You take things with you."

> "For the most part I learn on stage and from listening to records, which is real school," Ben-Ari said. "Every time I listen to music I learn. I never stop playing and I will always learn."

### Joining the Jazz Scene

After hearing the music of Charlie Parker, Ben-Ari began playing jazz herself. In the late 1990s she moved from Israel to the United States, determined to make a name for herself as a jazz musician. Although she studied for a time at the Mannes School of Music in New York City, she soon devoted herself to professional work. She played in orchestra pits for such Broadway productions as *Miss Saigon* and *Les Miserables* and in such jazz clubs as New York's legendary Blue Note. Ben-Ari also performed as a background musician with R&B singer Luther Vandross, guitarist Les Paul, and the singing group Manhattan Transfer. During this formative period of her career, she also found

*Ben-Ari with Kanye West performing at the American Music Awards, 2004.*

jazz mentors like trumpet player Wynton Marsalis. "When you're on the stage with a person like Wynton Marsalis," she said, "you just humble yourself, listen, and learn."

A chance encounter brought Ben-Ari together with the jazz vocalist Betty Carter, and soon the violinist joined the late singer's jazz education program, Jazz Ahead. "The whole idea behind Jazz Ahead," Ben-Ari explained, was "being yourself and not sounding like someone else." In 1998 they performed together at the Kennedy Center in Washington, DC. Ben-Ari credits Carter for teaching her "the importance of being original and the importance of not being afraid to be original. To stick to your guns with pride," she said. "You are who you are and that's it."

With her entry into jazz, Ben-Ari's reputation as a passionate, no-holds-barred performer grew. "Miri Ben-Ari plays the violin like her life depended on it," the *Village Voice* raved. She also completed three albums in short order. Her first, *Sahara*, was released in 1999 and featured all her own compositions. "The songs have clearly pronounced melodies," Jason Koransky wrote in *Down Beat*, "combining a decisively contemporary, funky sound with a jazz fiddle sensibility emerging from early swing and hot jazz."

Her next CD, *The Song of the Promised Land*, released in 2000, featured Marsalis on trumpet on two selections. Mike Joyce in the *Washington Post* praised the call-and-response between Marsalis and Ben-Ari on the album's title track. "Her impressive horn-like agility betrays her bop influences, and her Middle East background sometimes colors her tone and writing," the reviewer said of Ben-Ari. "Yet swing she does." Ben-Ari dedicated the album to the cause of peace in the Middle East. "Music is the biggest proof that you can take people from different backgrounds, and they can communicate with each other on a high level," she noted. "I wish that the Middle East would come up with some other kind of communication that can transcend this fighting." In 2003 Ben-Ari released a live album, *Temple of the Beautiful*, which was recorded at the Blue Note jazz club.

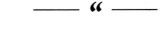

*"Nobody likes you the way a hip-hop audience likes you," Ben-Ari said. "It's so true and raw, the attitudes and emotions of hip-hop. This music is about soul, it's about truth, it's about honesty."*

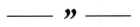

## Busting into Hip-Hop

During the period when Ben-Ari was recording her three jazz albums, she also worked as a studio musician and helped arrange songs for rap and R&B artists like Alicia Keys, Jay-Z, and Wyclef Jean. She soon found herself drawn to hip-hop. "Right away, I knew hip-hop was for me. It was all about being who you are and not being who you're not," she noted. "Sometimes when I play the violin, I feel like I'm spittin' a verse. I feel like I'm a rapper because I don't hold back."

Before long, Ben-Ari's unique "urban classical" sound helped her move from the studio background into the spotlight. She began writing, producing, and performing for such diverse artists as Allure, Dallas Austin, Brandy, Janet Jackson, Jay-Z, Joe, Patti LaBelle, Jennifer Lopez, Mya, Rahzal, Britney Spears, Thalia, 3LW, and The X-ecutioners. Over time, she built a solid reputation as a skilled and versatile collaborator. The challenge of blending her classical/jazz sound with the heavy percussion and strong vocals of hip-hop music appealed to Ben-Ari. "There are challenges in all types of music," she

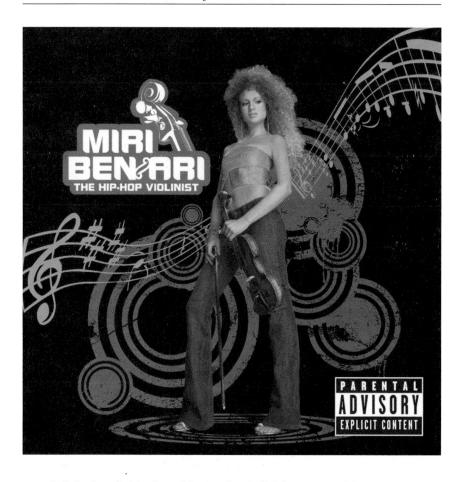

noted. "Hip-hop is hip-hop. It's not classical. It's not jazz. It's not pop music or bubblegum music. Hip-hop is its own unique genre."

Soon Ben-Ari began performing with popular rappers Biggie and Puff Daddy at venues like Carnegie Hall and the Apollo Theater. Her breakthrough performance on NBC's "Showtime at the Apollo" drew a standing ovation, and she followed up with appearances on BET's music shows "106 and Park" and "Rap City." Each appearance on the cable network drew unprecedented amounts of viewer correspondence, with fans demanding to know more about the "hip-hop violinist." Ben-Ari's subsequent appearance on Twista's hit single and music video "Overnight Celebrity" brought the musician even further into the limelight.

Among those impressed with the hip-hop virtuoso was Kanye West, who asked Ben-Ari to write, produce, arrange, and perform the strings on his blockbuster 2004 debut album, *The College Dropout*. The CD received both popular and critical acclaim, and its breakout smash "Jesus Walks" won the 2005 Grammy for Best Rap Song. Ben-Ari went on tour with West for sold-out performances throughout the country and appeared with the rapper on major television shows, including "The Late Show with David Letterman" and "The Tonight Show with Jay Leno."

Ben-Ari's energetic live performances have been described as legendary. "The way that I play," she said, "I don't hold back. When I get on stage, I give my hundred percent. There's something about hip-hop that allows me to do that. Nobody likes you the way a hip-hop audience likes you. It's so true and raw, the attitudes and emotions of hip-hop. This music is about soul, it's about truth, it's about honesty."

### Earning a Place in the Spotlight

How a classically trained Israeli violinist could be so naturally gifted in rap music is a mystery even to Ben-Ari. "Whenever I play, it just comes out like R&B and hip-hop," she related. "I said to my mom that I must have been black in a past life; it just comes to me. I don't even try. It's just sick, you know what I'm sayin'? It's like going to a foreign country for the first time and being able to speak the language." Ben-Ari claimed that growing up in the conflict-ridden Middle East provided her with a unique connection to rap music. "It's not easy living in Israel," she explained. "It's very rough, and there's constant struggle. And that struggle makes you stronger. That's part of what attracted me to hip-hop—it's raw, and the independent spirituality and philosophy behind it is part of who I am."

*"I don't hold anything back," Ben-Ari stated. "And that's my advice to young players. You might play classical. You can play jazz. You can play hip-hop. But whatever you do, let the world hear everything you have. Don't you dare hold anything back. That's the attitude that will help you succeed."*

In 2005 Ben-Ari released her fourth album, *The Hip-Hop Violinist*. It blends her strings with vocals from singers like Fabolous, Anthony Hamilton, Lil' Mo, Musiq, Mya, Pharoahe Monch, Scarface, and Twista. The project is "hard to explain," Ben-Ari noted. "There's nothing like it. The only thing I could compare it to would be Carlos Santana's projects, because he's an instrumentalist who mixes different elements like pop, rock, and Latin music. And I'm doing the same with classical and hip-hop."

Ben-Ari described the album's first single, "We Gonna Win," recorded with lyricist Styles P, as "a song of triumph. It represents my personal belief that with hard work, talent, and dedication, everything is possible. It's a one-of-a-kind marriage between rap and classical music, where the music doesn't accompany the vocalist, but rather stands on its own."

"One of a kind" is a term that has often been applied to Ben-Ari, as well. "When you create something totally brand new," she said, "there's no history. It's a lot of work, belief, and letting people know there's room for it." Reflecting on her eclectic "urban music" fusion of hip-hop, rhythm and blues, jazz, and classical forms, Ben-Ari noted that "Whatever kind of musician you are, you take everything you know, and you bring it to the music you are making. I don't limit myself to one style or form. It's just music. It's all good. It's all beautiful."

With concert tours and more collaborations in the works, the Israeli-born, classically trained, hip-hop violinist has shown the world she can stand on her own. "I don't hold anything back," Ben-Ari stated. "And that's my advice to young players. You might play classical. You can play jazz. You can play hip-hop. But whatever you do, let the world hear everything you have. Don't you dare hold anything back. That's the attitude that will help you succeed."

## HOME AND FAMILY

Ben-Ari, who became a U.S. citizen in 2003, lives in New York City.

## SELECTED RECORDINGS

*Sahara*, 1999
*The Song of the Promised Land*, 2000
*Temple of the Beautiful: Live at the Blue Note*, 2003
*The Hip-Hop Violinist*, 2005

## HONORS AND AWARDS

Grammy Award: 2005, Rap Song of the Year, for "Jesus Walks"
   (with C. Smith and Kanye West)

## FURTHER READING

### Books

*Contemporary Musicians*, Vol. 49, 2004

## Periodicals

*Billboard*, Nov. 20, 2004, p.67
*Down Beat*, Dec. 1999, p.56
*Interview*, Apr. 2005, p.70
*Jerusalem Post*, Feb. 24, 2005, p.24
*Jewish Week*, Sep. 21, 2001, p.45
*Miami Herald*, Oct. 21, 2004, p.E2
*San Luis Obispo Tribune*, July 13, 2001, p.3
*Strings*, Feb. 2005, p.43
*Syracuse Post-Standard*, Feb. 6, 2001, p.D4
*Vibe*, July 2004, p.82
*Washington Post*, Nov. 17, 2000, p.N9

## Online Databases

*Biography Resource Center Online*, 2005, article from *Contemporary Musicians*, 2004

## ADDRESS

Miri Ben-Ari
Universal Music Group
2220 Colorado Ave.
Santa Monica, CA 90404

## WORLD WIDE WEB SITE

http://www.miriben-ari.com

## **Dale Chihuly 1941-**
American Glass Artist
Creator of Such Series of Works as "Baskets," "Sea
Forms," "Venetians," "Floats," and "Chandeliers"

### BIRTH

Dale Patrick Chihuly (pronounced chuh-HOO-lee) was born
on September 20, 1941, in Tacoma, Washington. His father,
George Chihuly, worked as a meatcutter and trade union
organizer. His mother, Viola (Magnuson) Chihuly, was a
homemaker and later became a waitress. Dale had one older
brother, George Jr.

## YOUTH

Chihuly grew up in a working-class neighborhood of Tacoma. He developed an early love for nature by playing in his mother's garden and climbing a nearby hill to watch the sunset over Puget Sound. On weekends, his family would go to the Pacific Ocean and take long walks on the beach. Chihuly always searched the shoreline for small pieces of sea-polished glass. "Pieces of glass on the beach looked like gems to me when I was a kid," he remembered. "I was always fascinated with color and light."

Tragedy struck Chihuly's family during his teen years. In 1957 his older brother was killed in a Navy Air Force training accident. The following year, his father died of a heart attack. Chihuly's mother was forced to take a job as a waitress to support the family. Chihuly grew rebellious and became involved with a group of juvenile delinquents. At one point, he was arrested for throwing a brick through the windshield of a police car. He credited his mother—whom he once described as "industrious, encouraging, progressive in her child-rearing"—with keeping him out of more serious trouble. "If it hadn't been for my mother, I'd have probably been a bum," he acknowledged.

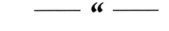

*"Pieces of glass on the beach looked like gems to me when I was a kid," Chihuly remembered. "I was always fascinated with color and light."*

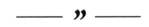

## EDUCATION

Chihuly graduated from Stadium High School in Tacoma in 1959. Despite a lack of interest in continuing his studies, he then enrolled at the College of Puget Sound. "I was never a good student," he admitted. "I only went to college because my mother told me I should." Chihuly did not originally intend to study art in college, but two events inspired him to turn in that direction. First, he wrote a term paper on the famous artist Vincent van Gogh. Second, his mother allowed him to remodel a small den in the basement of their home. Writing the term paper increased his interest in art, while remodeling the den taught him that he enjoyed creating and decorating space.

Once he decided to focus on art, Chihuly transferred to the University of Washington, where he majored in interior design and architecture. His academic career soon went off track, however, when he joined the Delta Kappa Epsilon fraternity and spent more time partying than studying. In 1962 Chihuly decided to take a year off and conduct his own art education. After selling the car his brother had left him, he traveled to Europe.

He spent time in Italy and France, then lived on a kibbutz (collective farm) in the Negev Desert in Israel.

The year overseas helped Chihuly become more mature. "I went from being a boy to a man," he noted. Upon his return to the University of Washington, he recalled turning into "a great student, kind of a worka-holic." Chihuly created his first artistic works involving glass during this time, by incorporating pieces of glass into woven tapestries. "I found I had to fire my own glass so I could embed wire into the glass to make it possible to weave it," he remembered. "The more I worked, the more the pieces became more glass than fiber."

After graduating with a bachelor's degree in interior design in 1965, Chihuly went to work for a Seattle architecture firm. Around this time, he began experimenting with glassblowing in his basement art studio. "One night I melted some glass between four bricks until it was liquid, then took a steel pipe and blew a bubble," he recalled. "It was kind of a miracle, because you have to get it at exactly the right moment. But it happened! Then I was hooked completely." Chihuly soon quit his job in order to explore his growing interest in glass art.

In 1966 Chihuly enrolled in the country's only hot glass program, at the University of Wisconsin at Madison. He studied under Harvey Littleton, who was widely considered the founder of the studio glass movement in American art. In 1962 Littleton had invented a small furnace that allowed independent artists to blow glass in small studios. Previously, glass work had required people to use huge furnaces in factory settings. Littleton thus helped transform glassblowing from an industry into an art form.

Chihuly earned a master's degree in sculpture from Wisconsin in 1967, then continued his education at the prestigious Rhode Island School of Design. While there, he worked with fellow student James Carpenter to create large installations involving glass, steel, and neon. Their most famous collaboration was "20,000 Pounds of Neon and Ice," which Chihuly reproduced at several exhibitions over the years. He earned a second master of fine arts degree in 1968.

## CAREER HIGHLIGHTS

Dale Chihuly is widely credited with turning glassblowing into a respected art form. The bold and innovative artist is largely responsible for expanding the basic concept of blown glass from small, decorative pieces to large, colorful sculptures. Chihuly creates glass objects in bril-liant colors and unique shapes that "dazzle the eye," "tantalize the mind," and "push the edges of art glass beyond anything made anywhere in the

## Glassmaking

The main ingredient of glass is sand, like that found on a beach. When sand is combined with soda and lime and heated to extreme temperatures (between 2000 and 2500 degrees Fahrenheit), it melts and forms glass. Glass exists in a natural form around volcanoes, and it may also be created naturally when lightning or fire occurs on a beach.

Humans first began making glass about 5,000 years ago in Mesopotamia, an ancient civilization in the area of the Middle East that is now Iraq. About 3,000 years ago, the ancient Egyptians learned how to wrap hot glass around a core of clay in order to make containers. The process of glassblowing originated in the Roman Empire more than 2,000 years ago. Like modern craftsmen, the Romans used a long tube to blow air into hot glass, creating a thin bubble that could be formed into many shapes and sizes.

Throughout its early history, glass was considered precious because it was so difficult and time-consuming to make. During the modern era, glassmaking evolved into a craft for the creation of functional objects, like ashtrays and candy dishes. This view changed during the 1960s, with the launch of the studio glass movement. The movement began when an artist and teacher named Henry Littleton developed a small furnace for melting glass. His invention allowed individual artists to create "art glass" in a studio environment. Before this time, most glassmaking had been done by industrial designers in large factories.

The process of creating blown-glass art begins when a blob of hot, molten glass is placed on the end of a five-foot-long blowpipe. The glassblower, called a "gaffer," blows gently through the tube to make a bubble in the hot glass. This bubble can be stretched and twisted into various shapes. The gaffer must reheat it every minute or two in order to keep it soft enough for molding. Once it attains the desired shape, the glass is cooled with fans or in special ovens until it hardens into its final form. Color can be added at various stages of the process.

world," according to Marilynne S. Mason in the *Christian Science Monitor*. His work is held in the permanent collections of nearly 200 museums around the world, and major exhibitions of his work often attract record crowds. "I call myself an artist for lack of a better word," Chihuly once said. "I'm an artist, a designer, a craftsman, interior designer, half-architect. There's no one name that fits me very well."

*Chihuly at work in his studio with a member of his glass-blowing team.*

## Learning and Teaching

After completing his education, Chihuly traveled to Venice, Italy, which has been a center of European glassmaking since the 13th century. He learned ancient Venetian techniques of glassblowing while serving as an apprentice to master craftsmen on the island of Murano. Upon his return to the United States, Chihuly joined the faculty of the sculpture department at the Rhode Island School of Design. He taught there for ten years and founded the school's glassmaking program.

In 1971 a couple of Seattle art patrons offered Chihuly 64 acres of wooded property overlooking a lake to build a glassmaking school. With the help of a number of fellow artists, he built the Pilchuck School of Glass on the site. Chihuly served as the first artistic director for the school, which attracted students and artists from around the world. "The impact of Pilchuck on the studio-glass movement, not just in the U.S. but around the world, is immeasurable, and Dale's contribution to that success is almost beyond description," explained fellow glass artist Benjamin Moore. "He has personally pushed glassblowing farther than anyone ever imagined it could be pushed, and his whole impulse is to share his knowledge with anyone and everyone he can bring together."

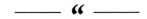

*"Chihuly's practice of using teams has led to the development of complex, multipart sculptures of dramatic beauty that place him in the leadership role of moving blown glass out of the confines of the small, precious object and into the realm of large-scale contemporary sculpture," wrote biographer Davira S. Taragin.*

## Losing Sight but Gaining Focus

In 1976 Chihuly accompanied a friend on a lecture tour of England. While there, he was involved in a terrible automobile accident. Chihuly was thrown through the windshield of the vehicle and suffered critical injuries. Doctors told him later that it took more than 250 stitches to repair his face. He ended up losing the sight in his left eye and sustaining permanent damage to his right foot and leg. It took nearly a year of recovery before he was able to work again. "You don't realize how much you depend on two eyes working together," he noted. "It's your depth perception that throws you. I couldn't pour water into a cup. Heck, I couldn't even walk properly. At first it was very disturbing."

Chihuly was determined to overcome his disabilities and continue his career as an artist. He began wearing a black eye patch and custom-made orthopedic boots. Since he wore the boots all the time—even when he worked—they became splattered with paint. "My shoes seem to soak up every spill and splash," he acknowledged. "I paint with a squirt gun, a mop, anything but a brush. Consequently, my shoes become more colorful every day." The eye patch and paint-splattered boots, along with a wild mane of curly hair, became his signature look.

Chihuly also had to change the way he worked after his accident. His loss of depth perception made it difficult or even dangerous for him to continue blowing glass. So instead of handling the blowpipe himself, he developed a team approach. Chihuly starts every new project by making a large, rough drawing of the object he wants to create, then discussing it with a hand-picked team of glassblowers. The team performs the physically demanding work of blowing and shaping the glass, while Chihuly presides over the operation, shouting directions and encouragement. "I had been blowing glass for a decade and when I had to give it up, I didn't really miss it. I had wonderful people on a team, and it was easy for them to work from my drawings," he noted. "In glass, there are lots of things you can't do by yourself anyway. It makes life richer to work with someone."

——— **"** ———

*"I call myself an artist for lack of a better word,"* Chihuly once said. *"I'm an artist, a designer, a craftsman, interior designer, half-architect. There's no one name that fits me very well."*

——— **"** ———

Chihuly was the first major artist to apply a collaborative team approach to glassmaking. Many people in the art world consider this to be one of his most important contributions. Working with a team allowed him to produce a large and diverse body of work, including many pieces that were significantly larger and more complex than he could have achieved working alone. "Chihuly's practice of using teams has led to the development of complex, multipart sculptures of dramatic beauty that place him in the leadership role of moving blown glass out of the confines of the small, precious object and into the realm of large-scale contemporary sculpture," Davira S. Taragin wrote in a biography for Chihuly's web site.

## Gaining Fame with Series

Chihuly is best known for creating series of works that center around a general theme. Each series eventually grows to include hundreds or even thousands of

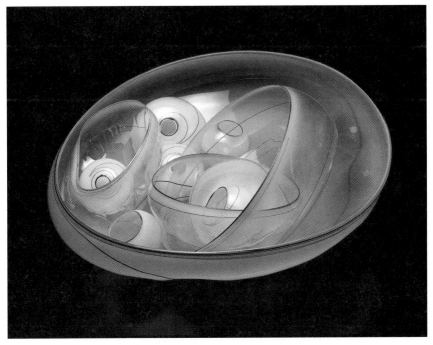

*Vessels inside of vessels are characteristic of the pieces
in Chihuly's "Baskets" series.*

pieces, which evolve and change over time. "Chihuly and his teams have created a wide vocabulary of blown forms, revisiting and refining earlier shapes while at the same time creating exciting new elements," Taragin explained. In addition to their distinctive forms, his works are also known for their vibrant colors. Bold reds, blues, yellows, and greens, as well as more subtle shades, infuse each piece so that they seem to glow with internal light.

Chihuly first came to public attention in 1977, when he launched his "Baskets" series. This series was inspired by the traditional baskets produced by Native American tribes of the Pacific Northwest. "I was struck by the grace of their slumped, sagging forms," the artist recalled. "I wanted to capture this grace in glass." Chihuly created about 100 pieces that were shown in successful exhibits at the Seattle Art Museum and the Smithsonian Institution.

Around this time, New York City's Metropolitan Museum of Art acquired one of Chihuly's works for its permanent collection. A number of other prominent museums and art collectors began commissioning works as well, and by 1980 he was earning enough money to quit teaching and focus all of his time and energy on his art. Over the next few years, his fame continued to grow and the prices he received for his works continued to rise.

Chihuly launched one of his most popular series, "Sea Forms," in 1980. These pieces were made using ribbed molds, which gave them a rippled appearance, and were adorned with long spirals of colored glass. "The 'Sea Forms' seemed to come about by accident, as much of my work does," he stated. "We were experimenting with some ribbed molds when I was doing the 'Basket' series. . . . Then the 'Baskets' started looking like sea forms, so I changed the name of the series to 'Sea Forms,' which suited me just fine in that I love to walk along the beach and go to the ocean."

> "The 'Sea Forms' seemed to come about by accident, as much of my work does," Chihuly stated. "We were experimenting with some ribbed molds when I was doing the 'Basket' series. . . . Then the 'Baskets' started looking like sea forms, so I changed the name of the series to 'Sea Forms,' which suited me just fine in that I love to walk along the beach and go to the ocean."

Chihuly's next series, "Macchias" (the Italian word for "spotted"), began in 1981. It grew out of his interest in using all 300 colors available to glassmakers. He typically used one color on the inside of the vessel and another on the outside, separated by a cloudy white layer in the middle. He also applied a ribbon of glass in a contrasting color, called a "lip wrap," around the edge. "Each piece was another experiment. When we unloaded the ovens in the morning, there was the rush of seeing something I had never seen before," he recalled. "The unbelievable combinations of color—that was the driving force."

As an indication of his growing international stature, in 1986 Chihuly became only the fourth American artist ever honored with a solo exhibition at the Louvre museum in Paris, France. Two years later he launched his "Venetians" series. Inspired by the decorative vases produced by Venetian artisans of the early 20th century, the series consisted of vase-shaped vessels covered with brightly colored strands of glass in the shape of stems, leaves, and flowers.

In 1991 Chihuly started one of his most ambitious series, "Floats." Its large, brightly colored glass spheres were inspired by the floats that Japanese fishermen once used to mark their lines. Some of the spheres reached 40 inches in diameter and weighed up to 80 pounds, making them some of the largest glass objects ever blown manually. "Even though a sphere or ball is about the easiest form you can make in glass, when you get up to this scale . . . it becomes extremely difficult," Chihuly noted.

In 1992 Chihuly expanded his vision even further with the "Chandeliers" series. These huge installations, which were usually hung from a ceiling or wall, included hundreds of individual pieces. In 1995 he displayed 14 of his "Chandeliers" over the canals and historic sites of Venice. "Chihuly Over Venice" also included more than 1,000 pieces by other glass artists. The million-dollar exhibition became the subject of a 1998 PBS documentary.

*Chihuly's "Sea Forms" pieces, with their characteristic ripples and spirals, grew out of his "Baskets" series.*

Another ambitious exhibition in 2000, "Chihuly in the Light of Jerusalem," involved 17 installations at the Tower of David Museum in Israel. First Lady Hillary Rodham Clinton invited the artist to design a millennium installation for the White House that year, and his work was also featured in a retrospective exhibition at the Victoria and Albert Museum in London.

After the turn of the century, Chihuly began focusing his attention on the interaction between nature and art. In 2002 he displayed many of his organically shaped sculptures at the Garfield Park Conservatory in Chicago, in an exhibition titled "Chihuly in the Park: A Garden of Glass." In 2003 he launched his "Fiori" series (from the Italian word for "flowers"). The "Fiori" are cylinders of glass ornamented with brightly colored petals, leaves, and other organic forms. Large installations can include hundreds of pieces arranged in a garden- or forest-like grouping.

## Creating Controversy

As his works gained worldwide attention, Chihuly built his glassmaking studio into a major business enterprise. The center of this enterprise is the Boathouse, a former factory on Lake Union in Seattle that serves as his home, studio, and office. He employs 200 people in various roles, including glassmaking, packing and shipping, and marketing and sales. Chihuly travels often for lectures and exhibitions, but he stays connected to his employees through a voice-mail system that allows him to leave messages for all of them at once. The marketing arm of Chihuly's business arranges exhibitions around the world, produces videos about his life and work, and sells prints and coffee-table books.

Over the years, Chihuly has provoked controversy within the art world. Some critics complain about his tireless self-promotion. Others dismiss his work as "craft," which is generally considered a less intellectual pursuit than "art." Chihuly's glass pieces and installations are very accessible to average viewers, and thus his work enjoys widespread popular appeal. In fact, it has been commissioned for the lobby of a Las Vegas hotel-casino and the dining room of a Disney cruise ship. But some people in the art world believe that works of art should be more challenging. "Chihuly's glass figures are pretty close to Everyman's notion of what art should be," Christine Biederman wrote in the *Dallas Observer*. "But by advocating a diet of nothing but eye candy, Chihuly compromises art's standards ever so slightly—a process that, in the end, leads us into temptation, into a betrayal of art's possibilities. He denies us the pleasure of being puzzled, of being intrigued or curious enough to sally forth into the books and learn."

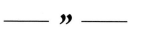

> "Each piece [in the 'Macchias' series] was another experiment. When we unloaded the ovens in the morning, there was the rush of seeing something I had never seen before," Chihuly recalled. "The unbelievable combinations of color—that was the driving force."

Such criticism does not bother Chihuly. He considers himself a populist when it comes to art, meaning that he wants ordinary people to like his work and is less concerned about what art critics think. "What I like to do is work on my work more than anything else," he stated. "It's varied in such a way that I can work on a chandelier, do a drawing . . . design a book, make some phone calls about an exhibition. That means a lot to me, being able to put it up in a nice way, and have a lot of people look at it, and really like it."

On a typical day, Chihuly gets up at four in the morning to begin producing sketches for his team of glassblowers. Although he maintains artistic control, he still tries to allow his assistants to exercise some creativity. "I

*Chihuly's "Macchias" are often displayed in groups that showcase the stunning use of form, light, and color.*

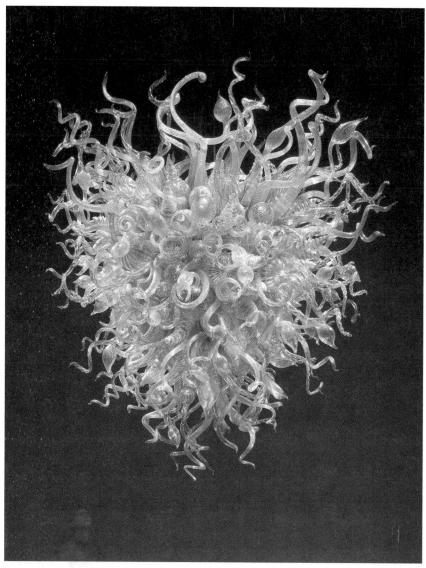

*A chandelier by Chihuly includes many interlocking pieces. No two are the same.*

rely heavily on the intuition of my craftsmen," he explained. "My job is to be a catalyst—to set the wheels in motion, keep the energy level high, and let things happen." They make all the individual elements of large installations in the studio and put them together. Then the sculpture is taken apart, packed into cardboard boxes, and shipped to the exhibition site, where it is reassembled. This complicated process means that no two exhibitions of Chihuly's work are ever exactly alike.

Throughout his 40-year career as a glass artist, Chihuly has maintained his love for the material. "I think glass is just a magical material that people appreciate universally," he stated. "You can't help but be interested in glass: Everybody is fascinated by the translucence and the colors. These are qualities that you cannot get in any other material—there are very few materials that are transparent. That means light can go through it, and it means it's possible to light it in ways that you can't light an opaque material. Also, I think glass is generally a mysterious material to people. The fact that it breaks makes it unique."

## MARRIAGE AND FAMILY

Chihuly married his first wife, playwright Sylvia Peto, in 1987. The marriage ended in divorce in 1991. He married his second wife, Leslie Jackson, in 2005. The couple was introduced by a mutual friend and dated for ten years before getting married. They have a son, Jackson, who was born in 1998.

*"You can't help but be interested in glass: Everybody is fascinated by the translucence and the colors. These are qualities that you cannot get in any other material—there are very few materials that are transparent. That means . . . it's possible to light it in ways that you can't light an opaque material. Also, I think glass is generally a mysterious material to people. The fact that it breaks makes it unique."*

Chihuly and his family maintain a residence in the Boathouse, the former factory on Lake Union in Seattle that also serves as his studio. Their home has several unique features, including a lap pool with a bottom made out of dozens of colorful glass pieces, and an 87-foot-long dining table carved from a single tree.

## HOBBIES AND OTHER INTERESTS

Chihuly collects vintage cars and motorcycles, Native American blankets and baskets, and handmade canoes. He also spends a great deal of time giving talks and demonstrations of his artistic techniques at schools across the country. In 1994 Chihuly and a friend, Kathy Kaperick, created the Hilltop Artists-in-Residence Program. This program takes at-risk kids off the streets of Tacoma and allows them to express themselves through art. "How could you not want to help young people?" he asked. "It gives me joy."

## SELECTED WRITINGS

*Chihuly: Color, Glass, and Form,* 1986
*Chihuly: Form from Fire,* 1993
*Chihuly: Projects,* 2000

## HONORS AND AWARDS

Louis Comfort Tiffany Foundation Award: 1967
Visual Artist's Award (American Council for the Arts): 1984
Golden Plate Award (American Academy of Achievement): 1994
Jerusalem Prize for Arts and Letters (Friends of Bezalel Academy of Arts
    and Design, Israel): 1998
Phoenix Award: 1998
Gold Medal Award (National Arts Club): 2002
Lifetime Achievement Award (Glass Art Society): 2003

## FURTHER READING

### Books

*Authors and Artists for Young Adults,* Vol. 46, 2002
Chihuly, Dale. *Chihuly: Color, Glass, and Form,* 1986
Chihuly, Dale. *Chihuly: Form from Fire,* 1993
Chihuly, Dale. *Chihuly: Projects,* 2000
*Newsmakers,* Issue 4, 1995
Vignelli, Massimo. *Chihuly,* 1997
Warmus, William. *The Essential Dale Chihuly,* 2000

### Periodicals

*Christian Science Monitor,* Nov. 30, 2001, p.20
*Current Biography Yearbook,* 1995
*Dallas Observer,* Dec. 20, 2001
*Forbes,* June 19, 1995, p.268; May 14, 2001, p.212
*Los Angeles Times,* July 20, 1994, p.A5; July 7, 2002, Sunday Calendar, p.6
*National Geographic World,* Mar. 1999, p.6
*Newsday,* Nov. 16, 1997, p.D28
*Norfolk Virginian-Pilot,* Mar. 28, 1999, p.E1
*People,* Dec. 13, 1999, p.117
*School Arts,* Mar. 1992, p.27
*Seattle Times,* Nov. 18, 1990, p.L1; Aug. 27, 1995, p.M1; Dec. 3, 1995,
    Pacific section, p.12
*Washington Post,* Nov. 26, 1978, p.K1

**Online Article**

http://www.chihuly.com/essays
  (*Garden Design Journal*, "A Glass Act," Feb.-Mar. 2002)

**Online Databases**

*Biography Resource Center Online*, 2005, article from *Authors and Artists for Young Adults*, 2002, and *Newsmakers*, 1995
*Wilson Web*, 2005, article from *Current Biography*, 1995

**ADDRESS**

Dale Chihuly
1111 Northwest 50th Street
Seattle, WA 98107-5120

**WORLD WIDE WEB SITE**

http://www.chihuly.com

# Dakota Fanning 1994-
American Actress
Star of the Films *The Cat in the Hat, Uptown Girls,
Dreamer,* and *Charlotte's Web*

### BIRTH

Hannah Dakota Fanning was born on February 23, 1994, in
Conyers, Georgia. She was the first of two daughters born to
Steve Fanning, an electrician and salesman, and Joy
(Arrington) Fanning, a homemaker. Her mother liked the
name "Hannah," while her father preferred "Dakota." They
compromised by giving their daughter both names, and she
eventually went with her father's choice. Dakota has a sister,
Mary Elle (known as "Elle"), who was born in 1998.

## YOUTH

Dakota comes from a very athletic family. Her father played minor-league baseball, while her mother earned a college tennis scholarship. From a very early age, however, it was clear that acting—rather than sports—was Dakota's first love. At the age of four, for instance, she often pretended to be pregnant by stuffing a blanket inside her dress. Then she would stage a dramatic play for her parents in which she gave birth to her baby sister.

When Dakota was five, her parents encouraged her interest in acting by enrolling her in a one-week drama class at the Village Playhouse in Atlanta. "My mom saw that [I liked to act,] and she got me with a playhouse where you study for the play and then do the play at the end of the week," she remembered. Amazed by her talent, the director told her parents to take her to a talent agency. Representatives from the local Hot Shot Kids agency were also impressed with Dakota's physical attractiveness and natural acting abilities. "I knew immediately she was a little prodigy and a child star," said talent agent Joy Pervis. "She has such a sparkle about her—she's a one-in-a-million kid."

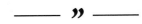

> *One of Fanning's first acting jobs was in a Tide laundry detergent commercial. "I didn't have any lines," she recalled. "I was just eating pudding, and then I spilled some on my dress. I had to do that about 20 times! But the pudding was really good."*

Hot Shot Kids sent videotapes of Dakota to their affiliate agency in Los Angeles, the Osbrink Agency. The owner immediately asked her parents to bring her to Los Angeles, where Dakota filmed three commercials in two weeks. The most prominent was a national Tide laundry detergent commercial. "I didn't have any lines," she recalled. "I was just eating pudding, and then I spilled some on my dress. I had to do that about 20 times! But the pudding was really good."

## EDUCATION

By all accounts, Fanning is intelligent and mature beyond her years. By the time she launched her acting career at the age of six, she could already read at a fifth-grade level. Her busy movie schedule prevents her from attending a traditional school. Instead, Fanning has a private tutor who travels with her to movie locations and teaches her at home when she is between projects. She has said that she'd like to go to a "normal, well, not 'normal,' but regular" high school one day.

## CAREER HIGHLIGHTS

### Breaking Through to Stardom

As soon as Fanning's commercials began airing on television, her acting career took off. Within a few months she was cast in small roles on several television series, including "ER," "Ally McBeal," "The Practice," "CSI," "Spin City," and "Malcolm in the Middle." Realizing that their six-year-old daughter had real potential as an actress, her parents then decided to move the family to Hollywood. Fanning made her film debut in 2001, at the age of seven, with a minor role in the movie *Tomcats*, starring Jerry O'Connell. Later that year, she received a larger role in the movie *Father Xmas*, which explored the true meaning of Christmas through the experiences of a family in wartime.

——— **"** ———

*In reviewing the movie* **I Am Sam,** *Kirk Honeycutt described Fanning as "an absolute angel with smarts—she delivers her lines like a seasoned pro."*

——— **"** ———

Fanning's breakthrough to stardom came in the 2001 film *I Am Sam*. Sean Penn starred as Sam Dawson, a mentally disabled single father struggling to raise a precocious young daughter (played by Fanning). Sam named his little girl Lucy Diamond, after the Beatles song "Lucy in the Sky with Diamonds." Since Sam's mental capacity is limited to that of a seven-year-old, young Lucy is forced to become the primary decision-maker in the family. As a team of social workers and attorneys tries to decide what is best for Sam and Lucy, Lucy is mainly concerned about protecting her father's feelings.

Both Penn and Fanning received a great deal of critical attention for their sensitive portrayals of the father and daughter. In fact, Penn received an Academy Award nomination for the role, and many critics felt that Fanning deserved an Oscar nod as well. In a review for the *Hollywood Reporter*, Kirk Honeycutt described Fanning as "an absolute angel with smarts—she delivers her lines like a seasoned pro." Fanning explained that the role came naturally to her because she has an aunt who is mentally challenged.

Fanning's performance in *I Am Sam* also received notice from several professional organizations. For instance, she received a nomination as Best Supporting Actress from the Screen Actors Guild. Only eight years old at the time, she became the youngest person ever nominated for an award

*Fanning with Sean Penn in a scene from* I Am Sam.

in the organization's history. Although Fanning did not claim that honor, she did win the Best Young Actor Award from the Broadcast Film Critics Association (commonly known as a "Critics' Choice" award), beating out Daniel Radcliffe (*Harry Potter*) and Haley Joel Osment (*AI: Artificial Intelligence*). When Fanning went on stage to accept her award, she found that she was not tall enough to reach the podium. Presenter Orlando Bloom had to pick her up and hold her near the microphone while she gave a surprisingly long acceptance speech.

In 2002 Fanning appeared in the movie *Trapped,* with Kevin Bacon and Charlize Theron. She played Abby Jennings, a young girl who is kidnapped. Fanning also appeared in the 2002 romantic comedy *Sweet Home Alabama,* playing a younger version of the movie's star, Reese Witherspoon. Fanning returned to television that year to narrate and star in "Taken," a 10-part, 20-hour science-fiction miniseries produced by Steven Spielberg for the Sci Fi Channel. The story covers more than 50 years in the lives of three families that are changed through their contact with extraterrestrials. "Ultimately all plot lines lead to Allie, a human-alien girl played with remarkable poise and intelligence by eight-year-old Dakota Fanning," Terry Kelleher wrote in *People.*

## Appearing Alongside Major Stars

In 2003 Fanning appeared in a live-action version of *The Cat in the Hat,* based on the classic 1957 children's book by Dr. Seuss. She played Sally

Walden, one of the two children who receive a visit from a mischievous cat (played by Mike Myers) while their mother is not home. Although *The Cat in the Hat* received generally poor reviews, Fanning enjoyed making the film. She especially liked learning and performing all of the physical stunts.

In her next film, *Uptown Girls* (2003), Fanning played a spoiled rich girl, Ray, who gets a new nanny, Molly (played by Brittany Murphy). Molly is the kooky, party-girl daughter of a late rock star. Her carefree personality clashes with that of uptight Ray, but they eventually come to an understanding. The nanny learns to be more responsible, while Fanning's character becomes more playful. "Ray belongs to a long line of precocious Hollywood brats, but Fanning ... displays the stellar presence and originality that made her so appealing" in earlier roles, Kevin Thomas wrote in the *Los Angeles Times*.

*"Twice in my career I can remember doing a scene and finding myself just watching the other actor,"* Denzel Washington said. *"Once was with Gene Hackman, and once with Dakota."*

In 2004 Fanning starred opposite Denzel Washington in *Man on Fire*. She played the daughter of a wealthy American businessman living in Mexico, and Washington played a former CIA operative who is hired to act as her bodyguard. The outgoing little girl helps the troubled agent open up, and when she is kidnapped he risks his life to save her. Washington—a highly regarded actor with an Academy Award to his credit—had high praise for his young co-star's performance. "Twice in my career I can remember doing a scene and finding myself just watching the other actor," he stated. "Once was with Gene Hackman, and once with Dakota." The role earned Fanning a Critics' Choice Award nomination for Best Performance in a Feature Film.

Fanning appeared in several films in 2005. She joined an all-star female cast—including Glenn Close, Holly Hunter, Sissy Spacek, and Robin Wright Penn—in the film *Nine Lives*. She played one of nine central characters whose lives intertwine in a series of vignettes. Next, Fanning decided to challenge herself by taking on a darker role. She played Emily, the troubled daughter of a psychologist (Robert DeNiro), in the thriller *Hide and Seek*. After witnessing her mother's suicide, Emily develops an imaginary friend named Charlie who begins threatening her father. Fanning wore a brown wig and dark makeup under her eyes to give her a spooky appearance in the film. "I had a really exciting time developing such a different character than myself," she noted.

*Stills from Fanning's movies:*
The Cat in the Hat *(top),*
Uptown Girls *(middle), and*
Dreamer *(bottom).*

Also in 2005, Fanning played the role of Tom Cruise's daughter in the highly anticipated action film *War of the Worlds*. Based on the classic 1953 story by H.G. Wells, the big-budget movie about an alien invasion received mixed reviews. Despite the early anticipation, many critics were unimpressed by the move. For example, critic Roger Ebert called it "a big, clunky movie containing some sensational sights but lacking the zest and joyous energy we expect from [director] Steven Spielberg." Others disagreed, as in this comment from Leah Rozen: "Fanning again proves herself remarkably gifted.... *War* is a sizzling summer popcorn movie offering two hours of solid story and gee-whiz, special effects-driven scares, all viewed from the comfortable safety of one's seat in a theater."

In *Dreamer*, released later in 2005, Fanning played the daughter of a horse trainer (Kurt Russell) who nurses a broken horse back to health and helps it win the Breeder's Cup. The movie was inspired by the true story of a horse with a broken bone that returned to racing: Mariah's Storm, winner of the 1995 Breeder's Cup. Fanning's role originally called for a boy, but producers eagerly made a change when they found out she was available. Fanning said that she "never really had any experience with horses" before the movie, but she learned how to ride for the part. In fact actor Kurt Russell, who plays her father in *Dreamer*, bought a special gift for her after they finished filming: he gave her a horse. "He's a palomino, and I keep him near where I live in California and ride him every weekend," she said.

Fanning has recently completed filming a live-action version of the beloved E.B. White book *Charlotte's Web*, scheduled to be released in June 2006. She plays Fern, with a stellar list of actors providing voices for the barnyard characters, including Julia Roberts, Oprah Winfrey, Steve Buscemi, John Cleese, Robert Redford, Cedric the Entertainer, Jennifer Garner, and André Benjamin, to name a few. "*Charlotte's Web* is one of my favorite books," Fanning says. "It's a dream part." After that, she will play the title character in two movie adaptations of the "Alice in Wonderland" books by Lewis Carroll.

**Trying to Stay Grounded**

Before even reaching her teen years, Fanning has become a force to be reckoned with in the entertainment industry. Since she made her film debut in 2001, her movies have outperformed those of most major actresses in Hollywood, according to *Entertainment Weekly*. Her movies have earned more than $600 million at the box office, which exceeds the draw of such stars as Julia Roberts ($586 million), Nicole Kidman ($497 million), and Reese Witherspoon ($338 million).

Despite her youth, Fanning has consistently received high praise for her acting skills. "She's incredibly talented and she has a wisdom in her expressions that belies her age," said Elizabeth Gabler, president of movie company Fox 2000. "She comes into your office, and after a minute you forget her age," added Adam Goodman, president of production at Dreamworks. "It's like being in a meeting with a really savvy, experienced film vet."

Fanning earns over $3 million per picture, and she receives more than 200 fan letters each day. Despite her wealth and popularity, insiders claim that she remains humble, polite, and remarkably normal. While she is often described as having an "old soul," she is also frequently called "sunny" and "fun." When a script calls for her to cry, she says that she remembers the night when her goldfish, Flounder, flopped out of his bowl and died. She also complains that the hardest part of acting is saying goodbye to the cast and crew at the end of filming. "You get to know everybody for so long, for two months, and then you have to say good-bye and then you're like, NO!" she explained.

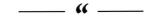

*Fanning complains that the hardest part of acting is saying good-bye to the cast and crew at the end of filming. "You get to know everybody for so long, for two months, and then you have to say good-bye and then you're like, NO!"*

To keep things interesting and challenge her acting ability, Fanning tries to alternate between "fun" movies and "serious" ones. She insists that she acts not for money or fame, but because she loves it. "From the day that I did the Tide commercial, I knew that I wanted to do this forever," she stated. "I can't even picture myself doing anything but acting. Acting is a real positive experience. We joke around, do some takes, and then have fun talking about it. Nothing is ever really hard. But it's always a challenge to take on a new character and stay in character."

## HOME AND FAMILY

Fanning lives in Los Angeles with her parents and younger sister, Elle, who is also a talented actress. She has appeared in *Daddy Day Care* with Eddie Murphy (2003) and in *The Door in the Floor* with Jeff Bridges and Kim Basinger (2005).

## HOBBIES AND OTHER INTERESTS

In her spare time, Fanning likes to knit, read, play piano, and ride horses. She also speaks Spanish and is an avid swimmer. Despite her adult career, Fanning insists that she has a "kid side" and still enjoys playing with toys. "When I go home, I play with my baby dolls and strollers and stuffed animals," she said.

Fanning also enjoys watching movies. Among her favorites are *My Best Friend's Wedding, Gone with the Wind, Titanic,* and *Steel Magnolias.* Her favorite actresses include Cameron Diaz, Julia Roberts, Meryl Streep, and Hilary Swank—"not just because they're great actresses, but because they are amazing people," she noted.

## SELECTED CREDITS

### Films

*Tomcats,* 2001
*Father Xmas,* 2001
*I Am Sam,* 2001
*Trapped,* 2002
*Sweet Home Alabama,* 2002
*The Cat in the Hat,* 2003
*Uptown Girls,* 2003
*Man on Fire,* 2004
*Nine Lives,* 2005
*The War of the Worlds,* 2005
*Dreamer,* 2005

### Television

"Taken," 2002

## HONORS AND AWARDS

Golden Satellite Award: 2002, for *I Am Sam*
Best Younger Actress Award (Broadcast Film Critics Association): 2002, for *I Am Sam*
Young Artist Award: 2002, for *I Am Sam*
Emmy Award: 2003, for "Taken"

## FURTHER READING

### Books

*Newsmakers,* Issue 2, 2005

## Periodicals

*Bergen (NJ) County Record,* Feb. 4, 2005, p.G8
*Entertainment Weekly,* July 29, 2005, p.10
*Orange County (CA) Register,* Jan. 29, 2005
*Orlando Sentinel,* Dec. 1, 2002, p.4
*People,* Aug. 25, 2003, p.75
*Time,* Mar. 7, 2005, p.76
*Times* (London), Jan. 29, 2005, p.22
*USA Today,* Mar. 6, 2002, p.D2
*Variety,* Jan. 31, 2005, p.48

## Online Databases

*Biography Resource Center Online,* 2005, article from *Newsmakers,* 2005

Additional information for this profile came from interviews with Dakota Fanning for "CNN Live Today" (conducted on January 30, 2002, and August 20, 2003) and for "The Today Show" (conducted August 7, 2003).

## ADDRESS

Dakota Fanning
Osbrink Talent Agency
4343 Lankershim Blvd., Suite 100
Universal City, CA 91602

# Russel Honoré 1947-
American Lieutenant General in the U.S. Army
Leader of the Military Response to Hurricane Katrina

## BIRTH

Russel L. Honoré (pronounced ON-er-ay) was born in 1947
in Lakeland, Louisiana. Lakeland is a rural community in
Pointe Coupee Parish, located northwest of Baton Rouge and
about two hours from New Orleans. His father was a subsis-
tence farmer, meaning that he grew crops and raised animals
to feed the family. Honoré has described his father as a
"master of provisions, of providing for the family."

Honoré was the youngest boy in a family of 12 children,
which included nine boys and three girls. According to family

legend, he was born during a hurricane: a 1947 storm that ripped across the Gulf of Mexico, killing 51 people in its path.

## YOUTH

Like many people from Louisiana, Honoré boasts a rich ethnic heritage. He has described himself as a "Louisiana Creole African-American." Creoles are descended from the original European settlers of the Gulf Coast region and share a distinctive dialect.

Honoré was raised in a close-knit family where everyone helped out on the farm. "I grew up poor, but we had a good family," he noted. They grew sugar cane, corn, squash, and cotton, and they also raised pigs and chickens. Honoré once won a 4-H contest with their only cow, Weasel. As a boy, he spent two summers living with relatives in New Orleans. He recalled playing in the streets of the historic city and listening to its famous blues and jazz music.

*"The Army gave me open sky," Honoré explained. "I got in the military and I liked what I was doing and the opportunity to be judged by your performance as opposed to other measures."*

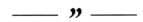

## EDUCATION

Honoré attended Southern University and A&M College, a historically African-American school in Baton Rouge. He worked on a dairy farm during his college years, and he also served in the Reserve Officer Training Corps (ROTC). ROTC is a leadership course offered in some high schools and colleges by branches of the U.S. military. A student completing ROTC in college can earn an officer's rank. College scholarships are available for ROTC participants, who pay back the scholarship by agreeing to serve in the military. Honoré earned a Bachelor of Science (BS) degree in agriculture in 1971 at Southern University and A&M College. Later, during his military career, he added a Master of Arts (MA) degree in human resource management from Troy State University in Alabama.

## CAREER HIGHLIGHTS

### Building a Military Career

After completing his undergraduate education, Honoré joined the United States Army. Thanks to his ROTC training, he entered the military as an officer, receiving his commission as a second lieutenant of infantry (ground troops). Honoré originally planned to serve in the military for a few years and then quit to become a farmer. But he soon found that he enjoyed the military and decided to make it his career. "The Army gave me open sky," he explained. "I got in the military and I liked what I was doing and the opportunity to be judged by your performance as opposed to other measures."

Honoré has held a variety of command and staff positions during his nearly 35 years in the Army. He served overseas in Korea and Germany, for instance, and was posted to Saudi Arabia during the 1991 Persian Gulf War. He also worked in Washington, DC, as vice director of operations for the Joint Staff (a group consisting of representatives from all branches of the U.S. military). He helped the Department of Defense organize its response to Hurricane Hugo in 1989, and in 2001 he commanded rescue efforts during catastrophic flooding in the African nation of Mozambique.

—— **"** ——

*Honoré welcomed the challenge of preparing the part-time soldiers— reservists and guardsmen— for the conditions they would face overseas. "I take this personal that we prepare every son and daughter to go fight," he stated. "We will have them ready. Failure is not an option."*

—— **"** ——

In 2002 Honoré was appointed commander of the Standing Joint Force Headquarters in the Department of Homeland Security, which was created in the wake of the terrorist attacks of September 11, 2001. In this role, he devised plans for the military response to terrorist attacks and natural disasters.

In 2004 Honoré was promoted to lieutenant general and given command of the First U.S. Army, one of two continental armies in the United States. He was assigned to Fort Gillem, Georgia, where all U.S. Army Reserve troops and National Guard units east of the Mississippi River received training before serving in Iraq and Afghanistan. As opposed to active-duty forces, whose main job is military service, reservists and guardsmen hold civilian (non-military) jobs, but they can be called up for active duty as needed.

Honoré welcomed the challenge of preparing these part-time soldiers for the conditions they would face overseas. "I take this personal that we prepare every son and daughter to go fight," he stated. "We will have them ready. Failure is not an option." Honoré employed a system called "theater immersion training" to expose the troops to realistic battle conditions. He built imitation Iraqi markets and mosques and hired

Iraqi-Americans to play the roles of villagers, religious leaders, and terrorists. He set up exercises in which the soldiers would face such dangerous situations as roadside bombs and rioting crowds. Honoré wanted to ensure that the training took place "in a tough, realistic environment" because "we're a nation fighting a war."

## Hurricane Katrina Hits New Orleans

Honoré soon faced a new challenge. In August 2005 a large tropical storm formed in the Atlantic Ocean. It reached hurricane force and received the name Hurricane Katrina. Katrina struck southern Florida on August 25, killing 11 people. It weakened over land but quickly regained

*Honoré speaking during a news conference, with New Orleans Mayor Ray Nagin looking on.*

strength as it moved across the warm waters of the Gulf of Mexico. On August 27 it increased in strength to become a Category 3 hurricane, with 115 mile per hour winds, and the National Weather Service issued a hurricane warning for the southern coast of Louisiana. By August 28 Katrina had grown into a Category 5 monster, with 160 mph winds. The National Weather Service predicted that it would cause catastrophic damage to the coastal city of New Orleans, and Mayor Ray Nagin issued a mandatory evacuation order for residents.

At that time, New Orleans was a city of about 500,000 people located at the mouth of the Mississippi River, where it flows into the Gulf of Mexico. Its location made it one of the most important shipping ports in the United States. Yet it also left New Orleans particularly vulnerable to hurricanes. Known as the "Big Easy," the city was mostly built below sea level. It was protected by a complicated system of levees (walls made of concrete and earth) that held back the waters of the Mississippi River to the south and Lake Pontchartrain to the north. This low-lying city is nestled in between the Mississippi River, Lake Pontchartrain, and the Gulf of Mexico. Some disaster experts have compared it to a bowl waiting to be filled with water.

On August 29, Hurricane Katrina made landfall just east of New Orleans, near Buras, Louisiana. By this time it had weakened slightly to a Category

*A satellite image of Hurricane Katrina on August 29, 2005, at 1:45 p.m.
It made landfall earlier that day, at about 6:00 a.m. near New Orleans.*

4 storm with 145 mph winds. A storm of that size packs the energy of a
10-megaton nuclear bomb exploding every 20 minutes. Katrina also produced a 29-foot storm surge on the Gulf of Mexico—the highest ever
recorded in the United States. The high winds and rising water in the Gulf
caused severe damage along the Gulf Coast of Louisiana and Mississippi,
knocking down trees and power lines, tearing off the roofs of houses,
blowing out the windows of buildings, and tossing ships onto the shore.
Honoré compared the storm to a military attack. "It was coming to New
Orleans, then took a diversionary turn toward Mississippi," he noted.
"Then it hit the city anyway, knocked out all of our communications, our
television. We were blind. It did everything an effective enemy is supposed to do. It was classic."

### The Levees Break

Destruction from the hurricane was severe, but initially it seemed
that New Orleans had escaped the worst of the damage from Katrina. But
the destruction was still severe, and it soon became catastrophic. On

August 30, a major levee broke and sent the high waters of Lake Pontch-artrain coursing into the streets. It flooded 80 percent of the city with a toxic soup of water, chemicals, sewage, and corpses.

An estimated 60 percent of New Orleans residents had followed the evacuation order and left the city before the hurricane hit. But more than 100,000 people had remained behind. Some of these people ignored the order and stayed in their homes and businesses by choice, but most of them were unable to leave. About 20 percent of New Orleans residents live in poverty, and the same percentage do not own cars. The city and state governments did not provide an organized system of transportation to help the poor, ill, and elderly evacuate before the hurricane struck. Many people who wanted to evacuate were trapped, with no way to get out of the city. Some of the survivors climbed into trees or onto rooftops to escape the flooding. Thousands of others made their way to designated shelters at the New Orleans Superdome and Convention Center.

——— **"** ———

*"[Katrina] was coming to New Orleans, then took a diversionary turn toward Mississippi," Honoré noted. "Then it hit the city anyway, knocked out all of our communications, our television. We were blind. It did everything an effective enemy is supposed to do. It was classic."*

——— **"** ———

Government—at the federal, state, and local levels—was slow to respond to the disaster in New Orleans. Much-needed rescue and relief operations were delayed for several days as various government agencies tried to decide who was in charge. The Federal Emergency Management Agency (FEMA) usually directed the response to natural disasters, but it had become part of the Department of Homeland Security following the September 11 terrorist attacks. Critics claimed that Homeland Security focused all of its time and money on reducing the threat of terrorist attacks rather than preparing for natural disasters.

As frustrated New Orleans residents waited for help, conditions in the city deteriorated rapidly. Desperate people broke into stores to find food, water, and emergency supplies, while lawbreakers took advantage of the chaos to steal non-emergency goods. The Superdome and Convention Center sustained damage during the storm and lacked electricity, water, or working toilets. The thousands of people stuck in these emergency shelters endured extreme heat, hunger, dehydration, overflowing toilets, and occasional violence.

*Honoré hit the ground running upon arriving at the
Louisiana Emergency Operations Center.*

## Leading the Military Relief Effort

On September 2, five days after the hurricane hit New Orleans, President
George W. Bush toured the area and acknowledged that the government
relief effort was failing to meet the needs of the city and its people. Shortly
afterward, he appointed Honoré commander of Joint Task Force Katrina.
In this position, the three-star general took responsibility for coordinating
the largest humanitarian relief effort in U.S. history. He led all military
relief operations in the city of New Orleans and throughout the Gulf
Coast region devastated by the hurricane. Honoré brought several important advantages to the job: he had extensive training in disaster management; he was a Louisiana native who could connect with the mostly poor,
black victims of the hurricane; and he was a tough, no-nonsense officer
who knew how to get things done.

Honoré arrived in New Orleans on September 3. After surveying the
damage from a helicopter, he realized that the city had suffered "a disaster of biblical proportions." He immediately took charge of the situation
on the ground, moving aggressively where many government agencies
had hesitated. His strong leadership helped restore order to New Orleans

and gave new hope and confidence to victims of the disaster. "He came off the doggone chopper, and he started cussing, and people started moving," recalled Mayor Ray Nagin, who had sharply criticized earlier government relief efforts. "I give the president some credit on this, he sent one John Wayne dude down here that can get some stuff done."

By the time Honoré arrived, a number of news reports had created the impression that the city streets were unsafe, filled with marauding bands of looters and violent criminals. As a result, some of the Army troops entering the city were fearful. Honoré immediately began working to change this impression. A CNN camera crew followed him as he stood on a New Orleans street corner and barked out orders to the troops. He continually told the soldiers to lower their weapons, reminding them that they were involved in a humanitarian relief effort. "Imagine being rescued and having a fellow American point a gun at you," he stated. "These are Americans. This is not Iraq." Honoré felt that the media had exaggerated reports of the violence and frightened people unnecessarily. He challenged journalists to assess the situation personally. "You need to get on the streets of New Orleans, you can't sit back here and say what you hear from someone else," he declared. "It is secure. We walk around without any issues."

> "He came off the doggone chopper, and he started cussing, and people started moving," recalled New Orleans Mayor Ray Nagin. "I give the president some credit on this, he sent one John Wayne dude down here that can get some stuff done."

After securing the downtown area, Honoré led the evacuation of survivors from the crowded Superdome and Convention Center. He acknowledged the frustration of people who had been stuck in the shelters for nearly a week. "By and large, these are families that are just waiting to get out of here," he noted. "They are frustrated. I would be, too." He also admitted that it was difficult for the Army to provide food and water to everyone in the shelters. "If you ever have 20,000 people come to supper, you'll know what I'm talking about," he said. "If it was easy, it would have been done already."

While his tough leadership was impressive, Honoré also demonstrated compassion for the suffering of New Orleans residents. "These were mostly poor people who didn't have much other than their homes," he explained. "We didn't pull anybody off those rooftops that said, 'Damn, I left my Lexus!'" Having grown up poor himself, Honoré said he could identify with the plight of the evacuees. "When it's hot, they're hotter," he stated. "When it's cold, they're colder. When the wind blows, they go over farther. And when a plague hits, they die faster." At one point, the general personally stepped in to help an exhausted young mother struggling to carry infant twins down the street in terrible heat and humidity. He ordered a soldier to carry the babies for her, and he helped her reach a military hospital ship for medical treatment.

———— **"** ————

*Having grown up poor himself, Honoré said he could identify with the plight of the evacuees. "When it's hot, they're hotter," he stated. "When it's cold, they're colder. When the wind blows, they go over farther. And when a plague hits, they die faster."*

———— **"** ————

Under Honoré's leadership, "the character of the relief effort [changed] from a mad scramble to an increasingly orderly and effective rescue and restoration," Patrik Jonsson wrote in the *Christian Science Monitor*. By September 19, 2005, the Army had delivered 13.6 million meals, handed out 24.2 million liters of water, and sent out more search-and-rescue helicopters than currently flying in Iraq and Afghanistan combined.

## Becoming a National Hero

For the duration of Joint Task Force Katrina, Honoré was based at Camp Shelby, Louisiana, about 100 miles north of New Orleans. He gave a press briefing there every morning and then traveled by helicopter to the disaster zone. He spent most of each day riding around New Orleans in the back of an army truck, assessing the relief efforts and assigning more manpower wherever it was needed. He returned to Camp Shelby late at night for another press briefing. Despite the hectic schedule, Honoré was glad that the military was able to help victims of the disaster. "We're usually in the business of breaking things," he said. "Now we're trying to fix things."

Honoré won over the media and the American people with his colorful press briefings, which were full of interesting metaphors and peppered with profanity. In one of his most famous metaphors, Honoré compared the hurricane and the relief efforts to a football game in which the home team must fight to overcome a big first-quarter deficit. "By definition, you're going to lose the first quarter in a disaster," he explained. "[But] what does the coach do when his team is losing 25-0 after the first quarter? Does

*Honoré quickly organized U.S. troops to help with disaster response at the New Orleans Convention Center.*

he call the quarterback over and tell him how stupid he is because he didn't play right, or does he get out the white board and start making adjustments? Now we can stay talking about the first quarter. All of you are talking about the first quarter. But there's still three quarters left to this thing."

Before long, Honoré emerged as the face of the disaster response. The gruff, cigar-chomping general known to troops as the "Ragin' Cajun" became an overnight celebrity. He received countless interview requests, and he appeared on several television news programs, including "Larry King Live," "Meet the Press," and "Face the Nation." "I can't swing a stick and not hit a reporter," he complained. "I didn't know there were so many of them." Honoré's aide, Lieutenant Colonel Richard Steele, noted that "The general is getting tired of all of these profiles. He's a humble guy. He didn't want to become a celebrity from all this. He wants the focus to be on the mission and not on himself."

By late 2005, the death toll stood at 972 in Louisiana and 221 in Mississippi at the end of house-to-house searches, and the insurance industry placed losses at $34.4 billion, making Katrina the costliest natural disaster in U.S. history. In the weeks after Hurricane Katrina, as the death toll mounted and the extent of the damage became clear, military and civilian sources alike praised Honoré's contribution to the relief effort. Some observers claimed that his performance as commander of Joint Task Force Katrina was likely to earn him a fourth general's star from President Bush, giving him the highest rank in the Army. "He's less a man than a force of nature," said one of his officers, Major John Rogers. "He knows the way and that's why he's leading."

> *"He's less a man than a force of nature," said one of his officers, Major John Rogers. "He knows the way and that's why he's leading."*

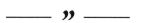

## MARRIAGE AND FAMILY

Honoré has been married to his wife, Beverly, since he started his military career. They have two daughters, Stephanie and Kimberly, and two sons, Michael and Stephen. Honoré and his wife live in Atlanta with their youngest, Stephen, who is still in high school. Stephanie lives in Florida and recently gave birth to Honoré's first grandchild. Michael is a sergeant in the Louisiana National Guard and recently completed a year of service in Iraq.

Kimberly lives in New Orleans, but she was out of town when Hurricane Katrina hit the city. When her father took charge of the military relief effort, she asked him to go to her apartment and rescue her cat. "I've got 80 helicopters in the air and we're trying to evacuate 20,000 people from the Convention Center, and she's e-mailing me every day about her cat," Honoré recalled. He eventually did make it to the apartment, where he found the cat healthy after ten days on its own. "The cat was living large in that place," he joked.

## HOBBIES AND OTHER INTERESTS

Honoré is an avid gardener, calling it his favorite form of relaxation and exercise. He grows pumpkins, tomatoes, beans, peas, potatoes, and peppers, and he shares his fresh produce with the Fort Gillem troops at barbeques. Honoré also enjoys the music of Tina Turner and B.B. King, and he wants to learn to play the guitar someday.

## HONORS AND AWARDS

Honoré has received numerous military awards, including the Defense Distinguished Service Medal, the Distinguished Service Medal, the Legion of Merit with Four Oak Leaf Clusters, the Bronze Star, the Defense Meritorious Service Medal, the Meritorious Service Medal with Three Oak Leaf Clusters, the Army Commendation Medal with Three Oak Leaf Clusters, and the Army Achievement Medal.

## FURTHER READING

### Periodicals

*Atlanta Journal-Constitution*, July 16, 2004, p.B4; Dec. 3, 2004, p.A14; Sep. 4, 2005, p.A13
*Chicago Tribune*, Sep. 9, 2005, p.A5
*Christian Science Monitor*, Sep. 9, 2005, p.1
*Inside the Army*, Sep. 5, 2005, p.1
*Newsweek*, Sep. 12, 2005, p.42
*Time*, Sep. 19, 2005, p.56
*Washington Post*, Sep. 12, 2005, p.C1

### Online Articles

http://www4.army.mil
   (*Army News Service*, "Troops Ready to Assist with Hurricane Katrina," Aug. 29, 2005)
http://cnn.com
   (CNN, "Lt. Gen. Honoré a 'John Wayne Dude,'" Sep. 3, 2005)
http://www.insightnews.com
   (*Insight News*, "Honoré's Peace," Sep. 20, 2005)
http://www.nola.com
   (*New Orleans Times-Picayune*, "Three-Star Celebrity," Sep. 19, 2005)
http://usinfo.state.gov
   (USinfo.state.gov, "Louisiana Native General in Charge of New Orleans Relief," Sep. 4, 2005)
http://www.washingtonpost.com
   (*Washington Post*, "Ragin' Cajun General Spurs Katrina Aid," Sep. 11, 2005)

### ADDRESS

Lt. General Russel Honoré
Fort Gillem
Headquarters, First U.S. Army
4705 North Wheeler Drive
Forest Park, GA 30297

### WORLD WIDE WEB SITES

http://www.army.mil
http://www.nationalveteransday.org/speakers/honore.htm

## Steve Nash 1974-
Canadian Professional Basketball Player with
the Phoenix Suns
NBA Most Valuable Player for 2004-05

### BIRTH

Steven John Nash was born on February 7, 1974, in Johan-
nesburg, South Africa. His father, John Nash, was a professional soccer player at the time of his birth. When his soccer
career ended, John Nash moved the family to Victoria, British
Columbia, Canada, where he worked as a marketing manager at a credit union. Steve's mother, Jean Nash, worked as
a special education teacher's assistant. The family also included Steve's brother, Martin, and sister, Joann.

## YOUTH

Thanks to his father's athletic background, Steve grew up loving soccer. In fact, his first word was "Goal!" and he received a soccer ball for his first birthday. Throughout his youth, Steve excelled in soccer, hockey, baseball, and lacrosse. But while his siblings stuck with soccer into adulthood (Martin followed in their father's footsteps to become a professional soccer player, and Joann served as the captain of her college team), Steve's life changed when he discovered basketball in eighth grade. He fell in love with the sport instantly and told his mother that he would grow up to play in the National Basketball Association (NBA).

In the mid-1980s, as Nash was reaching adolescence, the popularity of the NBA had spread around the world. At that time, the league featured a number of star players who were at the peak of their careers, including Michael Jordan, Isiah Thomas, Magic Johnson, Larry Bird, and John Stockton. Nash idolized these players and studied their moves endlessly. He watched training videos made by Thomas and Johnson and practiced four hours a day.

> "When I was in high school, I'd just dribble," Nash recalled. "If I was going to a friend's house, I'd just dribble. If we were going to play ball, instead of riding a bike, I'd dribble."

After a while, it seemed that Nash and his basketball were inseparable. "When I was in high school, I'd just dribble," he recalled. "If I was going to a friend's house, I'd just dribble. If we were going to play ball, instead of riding a bike, I'd dribble." Nash found a group of like-minded friends who would play pickup games at the nearby University of Victoria. "Me and my friends used to jimmy the doors [to the gym] so that when they closed up, we could get in," he admitted. "Friday night, instead of drinking beers at the beach, we'd sneak in and it'd be World War III and they had no idea. This was when we were 13."

## EDUCATION

Nash started high school at Mt. Douglas Secondary School in Victoria. By this time, he was already recognized as one of the best basketball players in his age group in all of Canada. After two years, he transferred to St. Michaels University School, also in Victoria. St. Michaels had an outstanding basketball team, and Nash made the move in hopes of advancing his basketball career. The one drawback to the decision was that he

*Nash led the Broncos to the NCAA tournament in three of his four years at Santa Clara.*

was forced to sit out his junior season due to rules governing transfers. During his senior season in 1992, though, Nash led his team to the British Columbia senior boys' high school championship.

If Nash had lived in the United States, his next step would have been simple: he would have selected from among the dozens of universities recruiting him, and he would have received an all-expenses-paid athletic scholarship to that school. But the situation was different for Nash because he played in Canada. "After high school, Canada doesn't really have a next level," he explained. "Not enough kids, not enough tradition."

Realizing that Nash's options would be limited if he remained in Canada, his coach at St. Michaels, Ian Hyde-Lay, launched a campaign to bring his star player to the attention of American universities. During Nash's senior year, Hyde-Lay wrote dozens of letters to the coaches of Division I colleges in the United States. He told the coaches how good Nash was and invited them to come see for themselves. "I wrote to everybody and heard back from nobody," Hyde-Lay remembered. "You don't want to stereotype it, but a 6-1 white point guard from Nowhere, British Columbia, was a tough sell."

Despite averaging an impressive 21.3 points, 9.2 rebounds, and 11.3 assists per game during his senior year, Nash was almost completely ignored by American schools. "The lack of a response hurt me," he later admitted, "because I thought I was good enough that people would come knocking on my door." Finally, though, one U.S. school did come knocking—Santa Clara University, located near San Francisco, California.

## College Years

When Hyde-Lay sent out the letters about Nash, he included a videotape showing the young guard in action during one of his high school games. Even though the video was grainy and hard to see, Santa Clara Assistant

Coach Scott Gradin could tell right away that Nash had talent. He showed the tape to Head Coach Dick Davey. "The first [video] was not the best quality, and the [opposing] players were not very good," Davey recalled. "I remember my assistant watching it and laughing, and I asked him what was so funny. He said, 'This video of a Canadian kid who makes defenders fall over.'"

Davey asked Hyde-Lay to send a second tape. After viewing this footage, Davey traveled to Vancouver to watch Nash play in the British Columbia senior boys' high school championship tournament. "About 30 seconds into watching warm-ups, I was looking around to see if [any other college coach] was there," he remembered. "You could just see the guy was special." After the game, Davey approached Nash and offered him a full basketball scholarship to Santa Clara. Nash happily accepted the coach's offer.

As soon as he arrived at Santa Clara, Nash became a "gym rat," constantly hanging out at the team's practice facility and working on all facets of his game. Davey described Nash as "easy-going and popular" off the court, but practically "deranged" in his dedication to basketball. It did not take long for Nash's spirit and enthusiasm to rub off on his teammates. "We'd practice all day, then he'd eat dinner and come back with five teammates to play 3-on-3," Davey recalled. "He made all the other players deranged too."

> *Santa Clara Head Coach Dick Davey described Nash as "deranged" in his dedication to basketball. "We'd practice all day, then he'd eat dinner and come back with five teammates to play 3-on-3," Davey recalled. "He made all the other players deranged too."*

Nash went on to have an outstanding career at Santa Clara that helped bring the Broncos into the national spotlight. He left college in 1996. It's unclear whether he graduated or left school without completing his degree.

## CAREER HIGHLIGHTS

### College—The Santa Clara University Broncos

Nash had an exceptional start to his basketball career at Santa Clara University. During his freshman season with the Broncos, he led his team to a coveted spot among the 64 colleges invited to play in the National

Collegiate Athletic Association (NCAA) tournament. Although Santa Clara was one of the lowest-ranked teams in the tournament, the Broncos stunned the highly rated University of Arizona Wildcats in the first round. Nash sank six free throws in the final 30 seconds of the game to seal the victory for his team.

Nash led the Broncos to the NCAA tournament in two of his next three years. During his senior season in 1995–96, Santa Clara entered the national Top 25 rankings for the first time since 1972. Along the way, the Broncos knocked off better-known and higher-ranked teams from Oregon State, Michigan State, and most memorably, the University of California-Los Angeles (UCLA).

*"The NBA is the major dream in my life and the grail I chase every day," Nash said before the draft. "I am obsessed with it."*

When Santa Clara faced UCLA in the season-opening Maui Invitational tournament in Hawaii, the Bruins were the defending national champions. Far from being intimidated, however, Nash looked around the locker room before the game and told the rest of the Broncos, "I can't believe a bunch of yahoos like us are about to beat UCLA." His statement gave his teammates the confidence they needed to claim a 78-69 victory. Nash scored 19 points while also holding UCLA's star guard, Cameron Dollar, scoreless.

The Santa Clara-UCLA game was nationally televised. Afterward, *Sports Illustrated* magazine ran a feature article about Nash. The little-known point guard from a small university had suddenly emerged as a nationally known college basketball star. Nash went on to average 17 points per game during his senior year and earn his second straight Most Valuable Player award from the West Coast Conference. By the end of the season, he was widely considered to be the top college point guard in the country, and it appeared likely that he would be selected within the first 20 picks in the 1996 NBA draft. "The NBA is the major dream in my life and the grail I chase every day," Nash said before the draft. "I am obsessed with it."

## NBA—The Phoenix Suns

When draft day finally arrived, Nash waited anxiously to see where he would start his professional basketball career. He ended up being selected by the Phoenix Suns with the 15th pick in the first round. Phoenix fans were not pleased with the selection, and those attending the draft actually booed when the Suns announced Nash's name. Many fans were unfamiliar with his game, since he was a Canadian who had played at a small college. In addition, the Suns already had two talented veteran point guards on the roster, Jason Kidd and Kevin Johnson, and many fans felt that the team had no need for another one. But the Suns had decided to select the best available player with the 15th pick, and management felt that player was Nash.

Playing behind two veteran point guards, Nash spent most of his first two NBA seasons on the bench. He averaged just over 10 minutes per game during his rookie season, then doubled his playing time to 20 minutes per game in his second year. Despite his limited minutes, Nash established himself as a solid outside

*Nash started his professional career with the Phoenix Suns, playing behind the veteran point guards Jason Kidd and Kevin Johnson.*

shooter, hitting an impressive 41 percent of his three-point attempts in his second season. He also learned a great deal by watching Kidd and Johnson. He absorbed tips from the veteran stars on distributing the ball to teammates while also controlling the tempo of the game. He also learned how important it was to play good defense in the NBA.

After two years, the Suns decided to make a trade in an effort to improve the team. In June 1998 Phoenix sent Nash to the Dallas Mavericks, a team that needed a starting point guard with three-point range. The trade turned out to be the best thing that could have happened to Nash. He signed a six-year contract worth $33 million, and he joined the starting lineup of an NBA team for the first time.

### Becoming a Starter for the Dallas Mavericks

Nash faced high expectations from the start of his career with the Mavericks. Unfortunately, injuries hampered his play during his first

71

two seasons with the team. He injured his foot near the beginning of the 1998–99 season, but he did not tell the coaching staff. Favoring the foot caused him to strain his lower back, which further limited his play. Soon, it became obvious to coaches and fans alike that something was wrong. Nash still made excellent passes to his teammates—in fact, he led the Mavs in assists, averaging 5.5 per game— but he simply could not shoot the ball well. In one game, he missed his first eight shots, and after that the Dallas fans booed every time he touched the ball. "That was the low point of my career," Nash remembered. "It had a huge impact. Half the time I'm confident because of the success I've had. The other half of the time, I'm saying to myself, 'You'd better work hard!'"

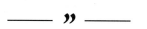

> "Half the time I'm confident because of the success I've had," Nash admits. "The other half of the time, I'm saying to myself, 'You'd better work hard!'"

The injuries eventually forced Nash to sit out half of his first season in Dallas. The 1999–2000 season did not turn out much better, as a right ankle tendon strain knocked him out of action for 25 games. On the positive side, he averaged a career-high 8.9 points in the games that he was able to play. In addition, Nash combined with young stars Dirk Nowitzki and Michael Finley to lead the Mavericks to the NBA playoffs for the first time in 10 years. Dallas lost in the first round, but it was still a huge step forward for the team.

During the summer of 2000, Nash decided that he wanted to represent Canada at the Olympic Games in Sydney, Australia. Before Nash joined the Canadian national basketball team, it was not expected to make it into the Olympic tournament. But as one of only two NBA players on the Canadian team, Nash became a leader both on and off the court and helped Team Canada earn a trip to Sydney. During the Olympic tournament, Nash helped the Canadians upset several higher-ranked teams— including Yugoslavia, Russia, and Spain—before losing to France in the quarterfinals, just short of the medal round.

Even though he did not win a medal, Nash gained a great deal from his Olympic experience. As the best player on the Canadian team, he had emerged not only as the team's playmaker, but also as one of its chief scoring threats. He averaged over 20 points per game during the Olympic tournament, and when he returned to the Mavericks at the beginning of the 2000–01 season, he was ready to raise his NBA game to the next level.

*Nash challenges Toronto Raptors guard Alvin Williams, 2002.*

## Elevating His Game

Finally healthy for the first time since the trade from Phoenix, Nash put together his best season as a pro. He nearly doubled his career scoring average to 15.6 points per game, and he also averaged a career-high 7.3 assists and 3.2 rebounds. In addition, he led the team in three-point shooting and finished fourth in the entire league in free-throw shooting percentage (.895). Observers agreed that the biggest difference in Nash's game was his increased willingness to shoot the basketball. "I needed him to shoot," said Dallas Head Coach Don Nelson. "He struggled until he got my message." Dallas made the playoffs once again, this time reaching the second round before losing to the San Antonio Spurs.

During the 2001–02 season, Nash's scoring average jumped to 17.9 points per game, and he was selected to play in the NBA All-Star Game for the first time in his career. The Mavericks made the playoffs again that year, but they lost in the second round for the second consecutive season, this time to the Sacramento Kings. Still, Nash's emergence as a star point guard made fans and teammates alike express optimism about the team's future. "We get along real well and we're winning," said his teammate Michael Finley. "Everything we worked hard for is coming together."

The Mavericks came out strong to start the 2002–03 season, winning 14 games in a row. Nash played in all 82 games that year and helped Dallas post the best regular-season record in the league, at 60-22. He averaged 17.7 points and 7.3 assists per game, set career highs for free throws made and steals, and was selected to the All-Star team for the second straight year. In the playoffs, Dallas knocked off the Portland Trailblazers in the first round. Then the Mavericks beat Sacramento in the second round to reach the Western Conference finals for the first time since 1988. Unfortunately, the Mavericks lost the series to in-state rival San Antonio, 4-2.

As the 2003–04 season got underway, many analysts predicted that Dallas would contend for the NBA title. The Mavericks acquired two new players during the off-season, Antoine Walker and Antoine Jamison. Together with Nash, Finley, and Nowitzki, the new players ensured that the Mavericks could put five All-Stars on the floor at one time. Unfortunately, the changes seemed to affect team chemistry, and Dallas never came together that year. Nash had another outstanding season, averaging 14.5 points and a career-high 8.8 assists per game, but it was not enough to lead Dallas to the NBA Finals. In fact, the team and its fans were stunned when Dallas lost to Sacramento in the first round of the playoffs.

### Facing a Tough Decision

The Mavericks' early elimination from the playoffs led to a number of changes during the off-season. Nash was in the final year of his contract with Dallas, which meant that he had to decide whether to sign a new deal with the Mavericks or become a free agent and sign with another team. Prior to the disappointing 2003–04 season, it was almost a foregone conclusion that Nash would stay with Dallas. But when the free-agent signing period began, the Phoenix Suns offered him a stunning contract—$65 million for six years—to return to the city where he had started his NBA career. Dallas made a counteroffer, but the best deal the organization could come up with was $51 million for five years. Nash found the Mavericks' offer insulting. "I thought they would come a lot closer than they did," Nash stated. "To me it was like they never really had any aspirations of keeping me."

The flamboyant owner of the Mavericks, Mark Cuban, claimed that the reality of the situation was that Nash never had any intention of re-

*Nash beats Tim Duncan to a loose ball during the NBA Western Conference Finals between the Phoenix Suns and the San Antonio Spurs, 2005.*

maining with Dallas. "It was Steve's choice to leave for the money," he said. "It was my choice not to pay him the money." In any case, Nash left the Dallas Mavericks after six seasons and rejoined the Phoenix Suns.

### Rejoining the Phoenix Suns

In Phoenix, Nash joined one of the most talented young teams in the league. Although the Suns had been plagued by injuries and finished the previous season with a disappointing 29-53 record, many observers claimed that the team was only one player short of being a contender.

Phoenix already had two of the NBA's most talented and explosive young players, center Amare Stoudamire and forward Shawn Marion. But without a skilled point guard to get them the ball, the effectiveness of these big men was limited.

With Nash on board, the situation improved immediately. "We went from not having a point guard to having a point guard," Marion recalled. "When you've got a point guard that's thinking pass first, everybody else just falls into place with that." "When you have a point guard who can pass as well as he can, it makes the game a lot easier," Stoudamire agreed. "I considered him the best point guard in the league when he was with Dallas. And, Steve's a great guy as well."

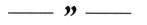

> "When you have a point guard who can pass as well as he can, it makes the game a lot easier," said center Amare Stoudamire. "I considered him the best point guard in the league when he was with Dallas. And, Steve's a great guy as well."

Nash was a perfect fit in Phoenix Coach Mike D'Antoni's up-tempo, fast-break offense. In order to be effective, it required a point guard who could make good decisions on the fly. Nash proved that he could do that and more in 2004-05. In fact, he had one of the best seasons ever by an NBA point guard. Although his scoring average dropped slightly to 15.5 points per game, he led the league by averaging an amazing 11.5 assists, and he led all guards by shooting over 50 percent from the field.

The addition of Nash helped the Suns stage a miraculous turnaround. By the halfway point in the season, Phoenix had already topped its win total from the previous year. The Suns went on to finish the regular season with an NBA-best 62-20 record, an amazing 33 games better than the previous year. The team's success surprised even Nash. "I certainly didn't think we'd be the best team in the league, record-wise," he admitted. By posting the best record in the league, the Suns gained home-court advantage throughout the playoffs.

Phoenix started off strong in the playoffs, sweeping the Memphis Grizzlies 4-0 in the first round. The second round saw Nash play against his former team, the Dallas Mavericks. He scored a career-high 48 points in Game 4 to help lead the Suns to a 4-2 series victory. In the Western Conference Finals, the Suns faced the powerful San Antonio Spurs. The winner of the seven-game series would play for the NBA title. Nash continued his spectacular play throughout the postseason, averaging 23.9 points, 11.3 assists, and 4.8 rebounds over 15 playoff games. But despite his strong performance, the Suns fell to the eventual NBA champion Spurs in five games.

### Winning the NBA Most Valuable Player Award

Although Nash was disappointed that his team did not make it to the NBA Finals, the end of the season did bring him a major consolation prize. He narrowly defeated center Shaquille O'Neal of the Miami Heat to win the NBA's prestigious Most Valuable Player Award. Nash received 65 first-place votes and 1,066 total points, while O'Neal gathered 58 first-place votes and 1,032 points. Nash thus became the first Canadian player ever to claim MVP honors in the NBA.

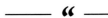

Nash knew that the award represented a significant milestone in his career, but he still felt a little uncomfortable about being singled out for his individual performance in a team sport. "This is the pinnacle of a player's career, individually, in many ways," he said upon collecting his trophy. "But the pinnacle of a player's career is also defined by winning. So 62 wins is as big a pinnacle as winning the MVP. That's the only reason I'm in this position. It's very important to me to make sure that my teammates know and the world knows this is due to my team's terrific character and camaraderie."

*"This is the pinnacle of a player's career, individually, in many ways," Nash said upon collecting the MVP trophy. "It's very important to me to make sure that my teammates know and the world knows this is due to my team's terrific character and camaraderie."*

To show how much he valued his teammates, Nash called the rest of the Suns up to the podium when he received the MVP award. To D'Antoni, Nash's actions proved that he deserved the honor. "It should be all about winning, it shouldn't be about anything else," said the coach. "What I like about it is someone being an unselfish player and . . . putting the team first and coming out on top. That's a pretty important message. You can score 15 points and be an MVP."

Basketball fans across Canada rejoiced upon Nash's selection as MVP, and the award cemented his popularity in the United States as well. Widely regarded as the best pure passer in basketball, Nash won the trophy because his selfless play made everyone on his team better. In

*Nash proudly displays his NBA MVP trophy, 2005.*

addition, some observers claimed that he and the Suns helped return the excitement to pro basketball. "A dash of Nash and his high-scoring Suns is just what the NBA game sorely needed," Sean Gregory wrote in *Time Canada*. "The pinball Canadian has almost singlehandedly put the fun back into the American game."

While the MVP Award brought Nash new recognition for his skills, he also receives a great deal of attention for his long, shaggy mane of hair. It has earned him countless female admirers—as well as male imitators—and the nickname "Hair Canada." Nash finds all the fuss about his hair rather amusing. "I really don't care what people's response is, this is just how my hair is," he laughed. "I don't take care of it, or comb it, or put anything in it, or style it or anything. When people comment on it, it is funny to me that it draws such attention. It makes me realize how insignificant that sort of thing is, how silly it is to get carried away by that."

## MARRIAGE AND FAMILY

In June 2005, Nash married his girlfriend of three years, personal trainer Alejandra Amarilla. They have twin daughters, Bella and Lola, who were born in November 2004. Nash loves everything about being a father, even getting up in the middle of the night to feed the babies. "It's hard when you get to the gym and you're exhausted," he admitted. "But when you wake up in the middle of the night to see those little suckers, it's the greatest thing in the world."

## HOBBIES AND OTHER INTERESTS

Nash is known as one of the smartest and most politically active NBA players. Off the court, it seems like he always has a book in his hands, and his curiosity about the world around him drives him to constantly seek out new learning opportunities. "I have a lot of interests," he admitted. "Books, music, current events, sports—I find things fascinating. I don't feel like I have to go back to school and become a professional student necessarily, but I like to learn."

Nash is not afraid to speak his mind when he believes deeply in a subject. Since the United States went to war in Iraq in 2003, he has not hidden his antiwar feelings. In fact, he created a stir at the 2003 NBA All-Star Game by wearing a T-shirt that read "No War. Shoot for Peace." "In Canada, we are very grateful and thankful for our relationship and many of the benefits the United States offers us," he acknowledged. "But I'm against war. I didn't take a stand against war to tell people how to think, or to tell them what to believe in, or to draw attention to myself. I just feel that in the present international state of affairs, it's important for people to educate themselves on what is happening so that they can make informed decisions."

Like many professional athletes, Nash tries to share his success by helping out with various charitable efforts. His main passion is helping to improve the lives of children, especially those who do not enjoy the advantages he had while growing up. Toward this end, Nash sponsors a 10,000-member basketball program for kids in British Columbia called Steve Nash Youth Basketball. "This is where I learned the game," he noted. "I wanted to say thank you. This is one way I can give back to the place that helped foster the development of my skills. I hope to encourage many more kids to love the game of basketball."

In addition to his work with the youth league, Nash operates the Steve Nash Foundation, which was founded in 2001 to support causes and events that encourage kids to live healthy lifestyles and participate in physical activities. He also purchases a block of tickets for every Suns home game and distributes them to local charities.

## HONORS AND AWARDS

West Coast Conference Player of the Year: 1995, 1996
NBA All-Star: 2002, 2003, 2005
All-NBA First Team: 2005
NBA Most Valuable Player: 2005

## FURTHER READING

### Periodicals

*Chicago Tribune*, Nov. 23, 2004, p.8
*Current Biography Yearbook*, 2003
*Maclean's*, July 8, 1996, p.12; Dec. 24, 2001, p.30; Mar. 10, 2003, p.48

*New York Times*, Aug. 30, 2003, p.D5
*Rochester Democrat and Chronicle*, May 8, 2002, p.D1
*San Diego Union-Tribune*, Apr. 24, 2005, p.C2
*San Francisco Chronicle*, Dec. 7, 2002, p.C1
*Sporting News*, Feb. 11, 2002, p.44
*Sports Illustrated*, Dec. 11, 1995, p.62; Dec. 17, 2001, p.102; Feb. 7, 2005,
    p.50; May 23, 2005, p.36
*Sports Illustrated for Kids*, Dec. 2003, p.42; June 2005, p.T4
*Time Canada*, May 16, 2005, p.46; June 20, 2005, p.42
*Toronto Sun*, Dec. 15, 1995, p.S12; Jan. 30, 2005, p.S14; May 28, 2005, p.S4
*Vancouver Province*, Dec. 13, 2004, p.A34
*Vancouver Sun*, Mar. 21, 2003, p.C11; Aug. 20, 2003, p.F1; May 9, 2005,
    p.D1; May 12, 2005, p.E2

Further information for this profile came from an interview with Nash
    for "All Things Considered," broadcast on National Public Radio on
    February 19, 2005.

## ADDRESS

Steve Nash
Phoenix Suns
201 East Jefferson Street
Phoenix, AZ 85004

## WORLD WIDE WEB SITES

http://www.nba.com
http://sports.espn.go.com/nba/players

## Lil' Romeo 1989-

American Rap Musician and Actor
Creator of the Rap Albums *Lil' Romeo*, *Game Time*,
and *Romeoland*
Star of the Television Show "Romeo!"

### BIRTH

Lil' Romeo was born Percy Romeo Miller on August 19, 1989, in New Orleans, Louisiana. His father, Percy Miller II, is the successful businessman, actor, and rap musician known as Master P. His mother, Sonya Miller, serves as vice president of Master P's record company, No Limit, and related businesses. Lil' Romeo is the oldest of their six children.

## YOUTH

Lil' Romeo's parents, who met in high school, once lived in the crime-ridden Calliope housing project in New Orleans. But they always knew that they wanted a better life for themselves and their family. "We didn't consider the ghetto home," Master P recalled. "We both wanted to make it out. We both refused to let the ghetto be a burden to us. We were just there for the time being, but we both dreamed of better things."

Just months after Lil' Romeo was born, Master P inherited $10,000 from his grandfather. He wanted to be sure that he invested the money wisely. First, he moved with his wife and young son to Richmond, California, to be near his mother. Once there, he and Sonya used the money to open the No Limit record store, which sold rap and hip-hop music at cheap prices. Within six months, the store was earning almost $10,000 per month.

> *"True wealth is not just about money," Master P explained. "It ain't about the music; it ain't about the movies. It's about family. It's about making a way out for them."*

After launching the successful record store, the Miller family moved back to Louisiana, where Master P used his connections in the music industry to start his own record company. Master P recorded several rap albums himself, and his No Limit label also released albums by other hip-hop and rap artists. The record company became yet another successful business venture for the Miller family. Within ten years, Lil' Romeo's parents had not only escaped the ghetto, but had become extremely wealthy. In fact, by the early 2000s, several sources listed Master P among the richest men in the United States, with a fortune estimated at $500 million.

Thanks to his father's success, Lil' Romeo enjoyed a privileged childhood. But his parents taught him to appreciate what they have. "True wealth is not just about money," Master P explained. "It ain't about the music; it ain't about the movies. It's about family. It's about making a way out for them." Lil' Romeo's parents often took him back to their old neighborhood so that he would understand where he came from. They also tried to set a good example for him by supporting charities that help the less fortunate.

### Following in His Father's Footsteps

Lil' Romeo learned to rap at an early age by listening to his father. Master P started his music career when Lil' Romeo was just a toddler. He formed

*Lil' Romeo with his father, Master P.*

the rap group Tru with his two brothers, Vyshonn (known as Silkk the Shocker) and Corey (initially known as C-Murder, he changed his name to C-Miller after a second-degree murder conviction in 2003). Lil' Romeo and his cousins often snuck into the studio when their fathers were recording. When Lil' Romeo was just three years old, he sang in the introduction to one of his dad's songs.

As he grew older, Lil' Romeo began recording his own rap songs. "Me and my cousin used to go in the studio while my dad was on tour and make our own songs," he recalled. "One day, my dad came home from a tour and the producer was playing our songs." Master P asked the producer who was singing, and he was surprised to learn that it was Lil' Romeo. Master P asked his son if he was serious about singing. When Lil' Romeo said that he was indeed serious, his dad decided to help him get started in the music industry.

## EDUCATION

Lil' Romeo is a straight-A student at Winward High School in Los Angeles, California. His favorite subject is math. Even though his successful music and acting careers keep him busy, he always makes time to study. When he is away on a concert tour or movie location, he hires a private tutor to help him keep up with his homework. "I do well in school because it's important to have your education," he stated.

Lil' Romeo learned the value of education from his parents. His father always encouraged him and his siblings to read by telling them it would help build the muscles in their brains. Master P also warned Lil' Romeo that he would put an end to his music career if he did not do well in school. "I always have to bring back an all-A report card," Lil' Romeo noted.

## CAREER HIGHLIGHTS

### Breaking into the Rap Scene

When Lil' Romeo began rapping as a child, Master P recognized his son's talent right away. His experience in the recording industry told him that Lil' Romeo had the potential to be a star. Lil' Romeo's songs were unlike most rap songs on the airwaves at that time, which tended to be full of violence, anger, and profanity. In contrast, Lil' Romeo's songs featured innocent lyrics and youthful subject matter that could appeal to people of all ages. The first rap song he wrote was called "Your ABCs"; he recorded it when he was only five or six years old. "I make music for the kids," Lil' Romeo said. "Grownups come to shows with their kids; that's a good thing. But I make music for everybody—kids, grownups, teenagers, everybody."

From the beginning of his career, Lil' Romeo has written all of his own songs. "I always write them or I won't feel like it's my song," he ex-

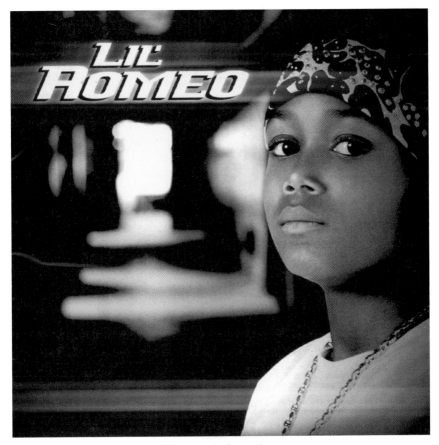

*Lil' Romeo's first release.*

plained. "I write all my songs and then my dad comes in and tells me what I need to change." Lil' Romeo also depends on input from his cousins. "I know it's a hot track when my cousins like it and start bouncing to the music," he noted. "If nobody bounces to the music, it's not [the] beat for me."

Lil' Romeo released his first album, entitled *Lil' Romeo*, in 2001. The first single from the album, "My Baby," made it to the No. 2 position on the Hot R&B/Hip-Hop Singles chart only six weeks after its release. At the age of 11, Lil' Romeo became the youngest artist ever to reach that position on the nation's music charts—breaking a record that had been held for decades by pop star Michael Jackson.

Lil' Romeo's debut album made him widely known among rap fans of all ages. His appeal stemmed not only from his musical talent, but also from his youthful good looks and outgoing personality. Violet Brown, director of urban music for Wherehouse Entertainment, said that the young artist "has it all—looks, personality, intellect, and talent," adding that *Lil' Romeo* "is an album parents can feel good about buying for their kids."

Lil' Romeo released his second album, *Game Time*, in 2003. It included such songs as "True Love," "Too Long," and "Clap Your Hands." Many of the songs on this album used pieces from older songs by such artists as Luther Vandross, Teena Marie, and KC and the Sunshine Band.

> ———— " ————
>
> *"I know it's a hot track when my cousins like it and start bouncing to the music,"* Romeo noted. *"If nobody bounces to the music, it's not [the] beat for me."*
>
> ———— " ————

Lil' Romeo's third album, *Romeoland*, was released in 2004. As the rapper moved into his teen years, he began to explore more mature subjects in his music. "On every album I try to talk about something different," he explained. "On my first album I focused mostly on myself. I was letting my fans get to know the real me. On my second release, I rapped a lot about my fans. I wanted to show how much I appreciated them. On this new one, I talk a whole lot about girls."

## Discovering Other Talents

Lil' Romeo's fame as a rap artist led to numerous guest appearances on television awards shows, talk shows, holiday specials, and game shows. He even played himself in a cartoon on the Disney channel. Lil' Romeo soon found that he enjoyed acting and had an appealing presence onscreen.

In the early 2000s Lil' Romeo branched out into an acting career. He starred in several television shows and feature films, many of them with his dad. Since 2003, for instance, Lil' Romeo and Master P have starred in the Nickelodeon family TV series "Romeo!" Although fictional, the show is based on the Miller family and shares many similarities with their real lives. Master P's character is a successful music executive whose name is Percy Miller. Percy is a single father with three kids of his own and a white foster son. Lil' Romeo plays the part of one of the sons, and his character's name is Romeo. The show follows the trials and tribulations of the family.

Both Lil' Romeo and his father enjoy working on the show, largely because it allows them to spend time together. "It's rare to see fathers and sons working together," Master P acknowledged. "You always hear about

*Members of the cast of the Nick show "Romeo!"*

black fathers not taking care of their kids. We spend a lot of time together doing this show. It's important to be with your kids. This show definitely involves family."

Also in 2003, Lil' Romeo played the role of Benny in the movie *Honey*. It tells the story of an aspiring hip-hop dancer and choreographer, played by Jessica Alba, who works in the inner city. She reaches out to Benny and helps him during his struggle with drugs. Mekhi Phifer and Missy Elliott were also featured in the film.

Lil' Romeo has also teamed up with his dad once in a movie called *Uncle P*. In this film, Master P again plays a role similar to his real life—a multi-millionaire businessman and rapper named P. Miller who lives in New York. His sister, a single mother living in California, becomes ill. So he agrees to move in with her to help take care of the kids. Although he has no experience with raising kids, he quickly learns the necessary skills. Along the way, he realizes that family happiness is more important that material success. Lil' Romeo plays the part of a rebellious teen who needs a father figure in his life. The movie is not yet released.

## Taking Care of Business

Lil' Romeo has also collaborated with his father in several business ventures. In 2002, for example, they worked together to create two lines of clothing: the P. Miller Shorties and P. Miller Signature. The P. Miller Shorties line features streetwear that appeals to children, while the P. Miller Signature collection is aimed at young men. Both are affordable for a person with an average income.

> "It's rare to see fathers and sons working together," Master P acknowledged. "You always hear about black fathers not taking care of their kids. We spend a lot of time together doing this show. It's important to be with your kids. This show definitely involves family."

Master P wants Lil' Romeo to be involved in his business ventures so that his son will have something to fall back on when his music career ends. "He's a natural talent, but I look at reality," Master P stated. "[The music industry] is a cutthroat business. But by me opening up other avenues and us owning this, we have independence."

Master P hopes that Lil' Romeo will learn enough to take over the business someday. "I want him to be able to take the business and run it successfully one day," he noted. "Just to have him educated and business-minded enough to know that your talent is what sells the music, but your business is what keeps it financially independent. I want to give him enthusiasm, and occasionally put him in the position where he can make decisions so he won't be afraid to make decisions once he has to run the business."

## Giving Back to the Community

Lil' Romeo's parents remember what it was like to be poor, and they both feel that they were lucky to escape that life. They taught their children about the importance of giving back to the community and helping people less fortunate than themselves, and Lil' Romeo took the lesson to heart.

In 2002, for instance, Lil' Romeo played in a charity basketball game that raised over $80,000 for leukemia, cancer, and AIDS research. Just a few weeks later, Lil' Romeo and Master P participated in an event dubbed "Game Time" at a video game arcade in New York City. About 180 needy or homeless children were invited to meet the famous rap artists while enjoying free food, drinks, and video games. During the holiday season, Lil' Romeo and Master P visit children's hospitals to deliver Christmas gifts to patients. "We've been very blessed, so it means a lot to visit these kids in the hospital and help them smile," Master P said.

Lil' Romeo also uses his celebrity to influence other kids to study hard and stay in school. In an effort to promote the importance of reading, he participated in Scholastic's Read for 2003. He joined many other celebrities to record messages that encouraged children, parents, and teachers to recognize the power of reading.

In August 2005, Lil' Romeo and his family were deeply affected when Hurricane Katrina devastated their hometown of New Orleans and large areas of the Gulf Coast of the United States. They had numerous relatives living in the disaster zone, and a home they owned in New Orleans was destroyed. The Miller family quickly came to the aid of hurricane victims. They formed Team Rescue, a relief organization that placed hundreds of evacuees in apartments around the country for three months. Master P also participated in a hurricane relief telethon on Black Entertainment Television.

*"There is a business side to this, but I wouldn't be doing this if I wasn't having fun," Lil' Romeo explained. "This is a lot of hard work for a kid. But I'm having fun because my parents keep me well grounded. This is just a hobby for me."*

## Staying Grounded

Despite the pressures that come with fame, Lil' Romeo enjoys his multifaceted career. "There is a business side to this, but I wouldn't be doing this if I wasn't having fun," he explained. "This is a lot of hard work for a kid. But I'm having fun because my parents keep me well grounded. This is just a hobby for me."

Lil' Romeo considers himself a normal teenager, and his parents try to make sure that it stays that way. "We dress average. We act average. We have rules in the house," Master P stated. "We have to wash the dishes, clean the house. We sit around and watch TV like everyone else. We try to stay as close as possible to regular." Since he thinks of himself as a regular person, just like his fans, Lil' Romeo always obliges people who ask for his autograph. "My dad taught me to always sign autographs and told me not to change because I was famous," he explained.

———— " ————

*Lil' Romeo's favorite hobby is playing basketball. "I always want to play basketball," he said. "That's my No. 1 outlet. I've been loving basketball since the age of two. Always basketball. You'll see me in the NBA real soon."*

———— " ————

Basketball is Lil' Romeo's favorite hobby.

## HOBBIES AND OTHER INTERESTS

Lil' Romeo's favorite hobby is playing basketball. "I always want to play basketball," he said. "That's my No. 1 outlet. I've been loving basketball since the age of two. Always basketball. You'll see me in the NBA real soon." Lil' Romeo plays on an Amateur Athletic Union (AAU) basketball team called the Texas No Limit Ballers. Master P, who is a skilled player in his own right, serves as the coach. At one point, Lil' Romeo was ranked nationally among the top 50 players in his age group. Among his favorite NBA players are Allen Iverson, Kobe Bryant, Shaquille O'Neal, Vince Carter, and Michael Jordan.

Like most kids his age, Lil' Romeo also enjoys hanging out with family and friends, playing video games, and listening to music. "I listen to everything—pop, R&B, rock," he noted. "I listen to good music." Some of his favorite artists include Bow Wow, Nelly, Britney Spears, *NSYNC, and of course Master P.

## HOME AND FAMILY

Lil' Romeo lives in Los Angeles, California. He remains very close to his family, which he considers the most important thing in his life. "Family always gonna be there," he explained. "The material things, they come and go."

## SELECTED CREDITS

### Albums

*Lil' Romeo*, 2001
*Game Time*, 2003
*Romeoland*, 2004

### Films

*Shorty*, 2002
*Pieces to the Puzzle*, 2002
*Honey*, 2003

### Television Show

"Romeo!," 2003-

## HONORS AND AWARDS

Billboard Music Awards: 2001, Rap Artist of the Year and Rap Single of
the Year, for "My Baby"

## FURTHER READING

### Books

*Who's Who among African Americans*, 2005

### Periodicals

*Baton Rouge Advocate*, Apr. 7, 2005, p.A15
*Billboard*, June 9, 2001, p.24
*Cleveland Plain Dealer*, Apr. 5, 2002, p.10
*Ebony*, June 2002, p.56
*Florida Today*, July 27, 2001, People, p.1
*Girls' Life*, Dec. 2004, p.42
*Jet*, Feb. 3, 2003, p.58
*Norfolk Virginian-Pilot*, July 17, 2002, p.C1
*Orlando Sentinel*, Aug. 4, 2004, p.D5
*People*, Feb. 10, 2003, p.59

### Online Articles

http://www.cbsnews.com
(CBSNews.com, "Lil' Romeo: Hip-Hop Sensation," Dec. 24, 2003)

http://www.mtv.com
(MTV.com, "Dave Matthews Band, Master P, Morgan Freeman Are also among Those Offering Help," Sep. 2, 2005)
http://www.usatoday.com
(*USA Today*, "Desperate Message Triggers Calls from across USA," Aug. 31, 2005; "Stars Roll up Sleeves for Hurricane Relief," Sep. 14, 2005)

## Online Databases

*Biography Resource Center Online*, 2005, article from *Who's Who among African Americans*, 2005

## ADDRESS

Lil' Romeo
Koch Records
740 Broadway, 7th Floor
New York, NY 10003

Lil' Romeo
Nickelodeon Studios
231 W. Olive Ave.
Burbank, CA 91502

## WORLD WIDE WEB SITES

http://www.nickelodeon.com
http://www.kidzworld.com/site/p829.htm

## Adam Sandler 1966-

American Actor and Comedian
Star of the Hit Films *Billy Madison, Happy Gilmore,*
*The Wedding Singer, The Waterboy, 50 First Dates,*
and *The Longest Yard*

### BIRTH

Adam Richard Sandler was born on September 9, 1966, in
Brooklyn, New York. His father, Stan Sandler, was an electri-
cal engineer, and his mother, Judy Sandler, was a nursery
school teacher. He was the youngest of four children in his
family. He has an older brother, Scott, and two older sisters,
Elizabeth and Valerie.

## YOUTH

When Adam was a boy, the Sandler family moved from Brooklyn to the quiet, leafy town of Manchester, New Hampshire. He grew up in a loving, supportive environment. According to his brother, Adam was "perpetually performing" from an early age. Both of his parents encouraged the side of him that loved to entertain. His mother often asked him to sing her favorite song, "Maria," from the musical *West Side Story*. When he was seven, she arranged for him to perform the song "Candy Man" for residents of a local nursing home.

Sandler's father was a jovial man who loved to laugh. He exposed his son to the slapstick comedy of such funnymen as Jerry Lewis, Mel Brooks, Abbott and Costello, and Rodney Dangerfield. From the time he was a little boy, Sandler would tell jokes and do impressions to amuse his parents and siblings. "He's always been funny," said his mother. "We knew he would be an entertainer. The only one who minded was Grandma Anna. She'd ask him, 'Why can't you be a funny doctor?'"

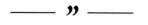

*"One time, my mother was yelling, 'Why don't you ever try?'" Sandler remembered. "I had a tape recorder in my hand. When she stopped shouting, I played it back to her. She laughed for half an hour. That was my life: doing something wrong, getting yelled at, and making the person laugh. Then it would be all right."*

Sandler continued performing music as he got older. When he was 12, he sang the Ringo Starr tune "You're 16" at his sister's wedding. "The first time I was ever on stage was at my sister's wedding," he recalled. "My mother threw me up there." His first song received polite applause, so he tried for an encore. "Things started to go downhill," he remembered. "'One was enough,' they said." Sandler went on to sing "House of the Rising Sun" in a seventh-grade talent show, despite the fact that his voice was changing and cracked throughout the performance. During his teen years, he played the guitar in several bands that he formed with his friends.

Sandler also continued to watch and enjoy comedy as he entered his teen years. He was a big fan of the late-night, sketch-comedy series "Saturday Night Live" from the time it made its television debut in 1975. "My big thing was trying to stay up to watch it," he recalled. "In the schoolyard the cooler kids were talking about it and I wanted to be part of that conversation." The release of the 1980 comedy *Caddyshack* proved to be a turning point in his life. He and his brother watched the movie over and over again and memorized all of the dialogue. "I have seen *Caddyshack* 300 times," he admitted. "It's the reason I got into comedy."

As Sandler focused more and more on being funny, he lost his focus on school and started getting into trouble. But he also found that comedy could occasionally help him get out of a jam. "One time, my mother was yelling, 'Why don't you ever try?'" he remembered. "I had a tape recorder in my hand. When she stopped shouting, I played it back to her. She laughed for half an hour. That was my life: doing something wrong, getting yelled at, and making the person laugh. Then it would be all right."

## EDUCATION

Shortly after his family moved to Manchester, Sandler started first grade at Webster Elementary School. For the first week or so, he became so homesick that he left school every day at recess. His mother always made him a sandwich and then walked him back to school. Once he adjusted to his new surroundings, he stayed in school all day and became a good student.

By the time he entered Hillside Junior High, however, Sandler found that he enjoyed fooling around more than studying. He became a class clown,

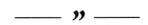

*"You've seen his movies?" said one of his teachers, Isabel Pellerin. "That's the way he was here. I can't believe he's making all that money for doing things he was punished for here. I thought he would grow up. Instead, he grew rich."*

willing to do outrageous things to make his classmates laugh. "Until sixth grade, I did really well in school," he said. "All of a sudden I said, ... 'I can't take it anymore. I can't read and be so serious in class anymore.' I don't know why, but I just started goofing off. Instead of being book smart, I decided to have fun."

As a student at Manchester Central High School, Sandler was a member of the drama club, served on the student council, and played sports. But he made the biggest impression on his teachers and fellow students by always getting in trouble. "You've seen his movies?" said one of his teachers, Isabel Pellerin. "That's the way he was here. I can't believe he's making all that money for doing things he was punished for here. I thought he would grow up. Instead, he grew rich." "Teachers would ask him to leave the class," recalled his principal, Bob Schiavone, "but they were

*Sandler with Kevin Nealon on the Weekend Update set on "Saturday Night Live," where Sandler got his first big break.*

laughing while they asked. He was hilarious." Despite his antics, Sandler earned respectable grades and graduated from high school in 1984.

As his high school years neared an end, Sandler considered his career options. "I had no idea what I wanted to do with my life," he remembered. "So I asked my brother what I should major in—he said acting, and that's how it started. I didn't know what else to do. But I love my brother, and I always thought he was smarter than me, so I thought I'd do what he said." Sandler applied to New York University (NYU) and, to his surprise, was one of only 300 students nationwide to be accepted into its highly competitive theater program, the Lee Strasberg Institute.

NYU's drama program trained actors to draw from their personal experiences in order to convey realistic emotions on stage. Sandler had trouble taking the classes seriously, though, prompting one professor to tell him that he would never make it as a professional actor. "I was a comedian in the Lee Strasberg acting program," he recalled. "Everyone else was pretty intense, whipping out the names of playwrights. We were all supposed to go on stage and dig out our emotions. At that time, I couldn't even look another person in the eye. I'm thinking, once I dig out my emotions, where do they go?"

Nevertheless, Sandler enjoyed his time at NYU. He formed close friendships with a number of like-minded students—including Tim Herlihy, Judd Apatow, Jack Giarraputo, and Frank Coraci—who later helped write, produce, and direct some of his movies. While still in college, Sandler also began to prepare for his future career. He took a year off to perform stand-up comedy in Los Angeles, and he also got his start on "Saturday Night Live" at about the same time. Sandler graduated from NYU in 1991 with a Bachelor of Fine Arts (BFA) degree.

## CAREER HIGHLIGHTS

### Performing Stand-Up Comedy

Sandler first performed stand-up comedy during the summer before he enrolled at NYU. While visiting his brother at Boston University, the 17-year-old took part in an open-mike night at a Boston club called Stitches. Sandler was reluctant to go on stage at first, but his brother talked him into it. "If he hadn't said to do it, I wouldn't have thought it was a normal thing to do," he acknowledged. "I would have said, 'Mom and Dad are going to get mad at me.' But because he told me to do it and I knew that my parents respected his brain, [I figured] it must be okay."

Even though Sandler's first attempt at stand-up comedy was not very funny, he immediately felt drawn to the stage. "It was the first time in my life where I said, 'All right, I think I can,'" he noted. "I became kind of obsessed with getting good at comedy. Growing up I wasn't that great at anything." For the rest of that summer, and throughout his college years, he took advantage of every opportunity to perform his stand-up routines in clubs and other venues. Although he found performing before an audience difficult and sometimes humiliating, it was all worthwhile when he made the audience laugh. "My friends were always around to say, 'Hey Sandler, you're funnier than that,' and that's what kept me going," he recalled. "They were always telling me I was a funny guy, and it took at least four years working in the comedy clubs until I believed it."

Sandler's comedy routines, as well as his confidence, improved steadily over time. He became the headliner at a popular New York club called Comic Strip Live, and he made contacts that helped him find other work. A friend introduced him to comedian Bill Cosby, for instance, which led to an audition for the hit family TV series "The Cosby Show." In 1987 Sandler appeared on four episodes of the program as a friend of Cosby's teenage son, Theo Huxtable. In 1990 Sandler took time off from college and moved to Los Angeles to test himself in comedy clubs there. He appeared at The Improv, a famous club where performers were sometimes "discovered" for movie careers. The year in Los Angeles helped Sandler develop a distinctive comedy style. "His act was not what I would call A-1 material," recalled Improv owner Bud Friedman. "It was more about his attitude, his little-boy quality, his vulnerability."

### Joining the Cast of "Saturday Night Live"

By the time Sandler returned to New York to complete his college degree, he had emerged as one of the most talked-about stand-up comedians working on the club circuit. In 1990 he was invited to audition for Lorne Michaels, the creator of "Saturday Night Live." As a longtime fan of the show, Sandler jumped at the opportunity. Michaels hired him to join the show's writing staff—a group of comedians who came up with ideas and created characters for the comedy skits that appeared on the air. The cast of the show at that time included Chris Rock, David Spade, and Chris Farley.

The first sketch written by Sandler appeared on the air on December 8, 1990. He recalled how nervous he felt as he waited backstage: "Sitting with [guest host] Tom Hanks ten seconds before the lights come up on my first skit on the air, I said, 'I might faint. There is a good chance I'm going to faint.' Hanks looks over, real concerned, and says, 'Well, don't.'"

In 1991 Sandler was promoted to "featured player," meaning that he appeared in occasional skits but was not part of the regular cast. He finally became a full-fledged cast member during the 1993-1994 season. During his time on "Saturday Night Live," Sandler created several characters that became pop culture icons. One of his most famous characters was Opera Man, who would dress up in robes and provide a singing summary of current news stories. He also created Cajun Man, who spoke with such a thick accent that no one could understand him, and did impressions of numerous rock stars, like Eddie Vedder, Axl Rose, and Bruce Springsteen.

Sandler made his final appearance on "Saturday Night Live" on May 13, 1995. It remains unclear whether he quit to pursue a movie career or was fired so that the show—which was widely criticized during his tenure for not being very funny—could go in another direction. "I loved being on that show, I loved getting to do my stuff every Saturday night, do something new, and see these bands and these celebrity hosts. It was great," Sandler stated. But he also admitted that, after five years on the show, he started to feel like he was repeating himself. "I didn't want to do that," he said. "I wanted to get into growing as much as I can."

*"There's just something really safe and likeable about seeing this guy up there," said comedian David Spade. "Even if you're only five years old, you poke your friend and say, 'At least I'm not as dumb as that idiot!'"*

## Making Comedy Albums

In 1993, during his time on "Saturday Night Live," Sandler released his first comedy album, *They're All Gonna Laugh at You.* Full of rude humor and foul language, it became a huge hit. It sold three million copies and was even nominated for a Grammy Award as Best Comedy Album.

In 1996, shortly after leaving "Saturday Night Live," Sandler released a second album, *What the Hell Happened to Me?* In addition to numerous comedy routines, this album featured "The Hanukkah Song," which became one of the most-requested songs of the holiday season. Drawn from his own experience growing up as one of the few Jewish kids in Manchester, the humorous song lists the names of celebrities who celebrate the holiday.

Sandler continued making occasional comedy albums as his movie career took off, releasing *What's Your Name?* in 1997 and *Stan and Judy's Kid* the following year. He released his fifth album, *Shhh ... Don't Tell,* in 2004. Sandler viewed the albums as an opportunity to cut loose with profanity and dirty jokes that he could not include in his movies. Although the albums carry strict warning labels to keep them out of reach of children, together they have sold more than five million copies.

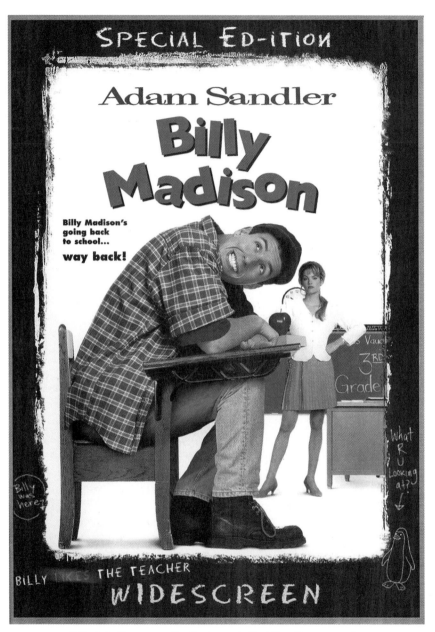

Billy Madison *was the first movie that Sandler co-wrote, and his first big movie success.*

## Becoming a Movie Star

In addition to making comedy albums, Sandler also had small roles in several movies during his years on "Saturday Night Live." He made his big-screen debut in *Shakes the Clown,* a 1991 comedy about the strange world of adults who make a living by appearing as clowns at children's parties. Sandler played Dink, the sad clown. The movie disappeared quickly from theaters, but later earned a cult following on video. He also appeared in *The Coneheads,* a poorly received 1993 comedy adapted from a popular "Saturday Night Live" skit. He played a larger role in *Airheads,* a 1994 comedy about three heavy-metal musicians who inadvertently take over a radio station.

As his time on "Saturday Night Live" drew to a close, Sandler began writing a movie script with his college friend Tim Herlihy. This effort turned into the 1995 comedy *Billy Madison.* Sandler starred as Billy, a good-natured but lazy young man who is forced to repeat his entire education—kindergarten through high school—in six months in order to collect a large inheritance. In *Billy Madison,* Sandler created the "loveable loser" persona that he returned to often in his later films. "He's like a big lug who can't get things right," explained his childhood hero, Rodney Dangerfield. "At the end of the movie, when he gets things right, the audience loves him. When he wins, he wins for everybody."

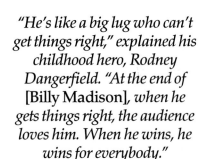

*"He's like a big lug who can't get things right," explained his childhood hero, Rodney Dangerfield. "At the end of [Billy Madison], when he gets things right, the audience loves him. When he wins, he wins for everybody."*

Although critics panned the movie, it did well at the box office and became a cult hit on video. Indeed, the movie also initiated what has since become the typical response to the opening of Adam Sandler movies: while many critics disparage his movies, his audiences love them, seeing them in theaters and then watching them repeatedly on video.

Sandler and Herlihy collaborated again the following year to write and produce *Happy Gilmore.* Sandler played the title character, a former hockey star with a violent temper. When he accidentally discovers that he can use his wicked slap shot to drive a golf ball, Happy enters a golf tournament in hopes of winning enough money to pay the overdue taxes on his grandmother's house. He causes trouble in the stodgy world of golf with his outbursts and fighting. Shot on a $12 million budget, *Happy Gilmore* earned a respectable $40 million at the box office. Although many critics dismissed it, a few found it amusing. "It's sort of like a Gen-X *Caddyshack*," Michael Sauter wrote in *Entertainment Weekly*, "with some good, punchy slapstick and delightfully sick twists."

The success of these two early films helped turn Sandler into a box-office draw. Audiences enjoyed his brand of humor, but the print media generally presented him in a negative way, criticizing both his acting and his writing abilities. "When I first read a bad thing about me," he recalled, "I was like, 'Oh, that doesn't feel very good, why should I read this anymore?'" Around this time, Sandler stopped giving interviews to newspapers and magazines. He focused all of his promotional appearances on TV and radio talk shows, where he felt that his words were less likely to be taken out of context. "The press really didn't give him any respect," said his friend and fellow comedian Chris Rock. "Everybody dissed him, and it's like, 'Now you want me to talk to you?' If I were him, I wouldn't talk either."

## Playing the Romantic Lead

The first role that earned Sandler critical praise came in the 1998 romantic comedy *The Wedding Singer*. He played Robbie Hart, a sweet-natured man forced to give up his dream of becoming a rock star and settle for singing at weddings and bar mitzvahs at a local banquet hall. After being left at the altar by his fiancée, he falls in love with a waitress, played by Drew Barrymore, who is engaged to a cad. Although the film did include some slapstick moments, the romantic leading man role was a departure for Sandler. It won him new fans among young women—which helped *The Wedding Singer* make an impressive $80 million at the box office— and also earned favorable reviews from critics. "A spirited, funny, and warm saga, the picture serves up Sandler and Drew Barrymore in a new way that enhances their most winning qualities," Leonard Klady wrote in *Variety*. "The candy-colored movie generates a fair amount of good will, especially when Sandler is singing," Jami Bernard added in the *New York Daily News*.

Many reviewers commented on the chemistry between Sandler and Barrymore, and indeed, his costar was pretty effusive in her praise. "Adam is amazing—he's one of the most incredible men in the world," Barrymore enthused. "He makes you laugh by combining humor and intellect, which to me is the most important combination I think a human being can attain. Someone who can do that makes you happy; they're like medicine. I worship comedians."

*Scenes from some of Sandler's hit movies:* The Wedding Singer *(top),* Happy Gilmore *(middle), and* Big Daddy *(bottom).*

Later in 1998, Sandler returned to his previous formula for success in *The Waterboy*. He played Bobby Boucher, a good-hearted dunce who works as the waterboy for a college football team. But the players use him as a tackling dummy, and he is fired by the coach. Angry, Bobby moves to another team, where his out-of-control rages turn him into a star offensive tackle. Despite poor reviews, *The Waterboy* became a huge hit. It earned a non-summer record of $39.4 million in its opening weekend and went on to take in an amazing $161 million during its theatrical run. "I had the best time making this—I got to hang out with my buddies, throw a football around, and I had a lot of fun tackling people," he said. "It was fun pretending I was tough. In real life I'm nothing. I have no fighting skills. If you wanted to hit me, I wouldn't do anything about it. I'd just cry like a baby. In fact," he joked, "I'm gonna go find my mom now."

> *"I had the best time making [The Waterboy]— I got to hang out with my buddies, throw a football around, and I had a lot of fun tackling people," Sandler said. "It was fun pretending I was tough. In real life I'm nothing. I have no fighting skills. If you wanted to hit me, I wouldn't do anything about it. I'd just cry like a baby."*

Until this point, many of Sandler's comedies had followed a similar path—except, perhaps, for *The Wedding Singer*. As Richard Corliss explained in *Time* magazine, "[The typical Sandler comedy] is about a nerdy sociopath who learns to channel his rage into an acceptable format: winning a spelling bee, playing golf, or tackling football players 'You don't have what they call the social skills,' he is told in *The Waterboy*; that is Sandler's gimmick and, for many, his charm. The plot is a competition for which our hero is unqualified but which he always wins, over some smarmy exemplar of the status quo and in a climax tinged with sentiment and demagoguery."

But with his next movie, Sandler began to move away from that path. In *Big Daddy* (1999), he played Sonny Koufax, an immature underachiever whose girlfriend dumps him because he won't grow up. So when his roommate's son shows up, needing a home, Sonny agrees to take care of him—just so he can convince his girlfriend that he can be responsible. Instead, Sonny ends up teaching the boy all sorts of bad habits—like how to pee in public, put sticks in the paths of inline skaters to watch them fall, and smash canned goods at the supermarket to get a discount on damaged goods. As their relationship grows, though, Sandler managed to infuse both humor and sweetness into the story. "There's a good amount of toilet humor but it's overshadowed by the sheer quirkiness of the script. It's just plain fun to watch a goofy man-child interact with a child," wrote reviewer Tom Grabon. "*Big Daddy* is easily the most heartfelt of Sandler's films." As before, the film received generally poor reviews but performed well at the box office, earning an amazing $163 million.

Sandler's next big hit came in 2002, when he appeared in *Mr. Deeds*. Based on an old Frank Capra film called *Mr. Deeds Goes to Town*, it tells the story of an unassuming man who suddenly inherits a fortune. Sandler starred as Longfellow Deeds, a happily dysfunctional pizza delivery boy who inherits $40 billion and has to figure out how to spend it. He travels to New York, where unscrupulous people try to take advantage of him, but he manages to evade their schemes through utter cluelessness. Although many critics, like Owen Gleiberman of *Entertainment Weekly*, complained that Sandler was "running on empty, repeating what he's already done way too often," the movie nevertheless earned $126 million at the box office.

Also in 2002, Sandler stretched his acting ability by playing a dramatic role in *Punch-Drunk Love*, directed by Paul Thomas Anderson. Sandler starred as Barry Egan, a painfully shy and insecure salesman who collects airline reward miles in hopes of someday escaping from his mundane life. When he meets a beautiful but mysterious woman, he must break out of his shell to win her over. Unlike Sandler's previous efforts, the film earned a great deal of critical acclaim but only generated $17.8 million at the box office. Gleiberman described *Punch-Drunk Love* as a "deeply rich and strange new romantic comedy" and called Sandler "utterly winning to watch."

### Expanding His Range

Sandler scored yet another box-office smash in 2003 with *Anger Management*, which earned $134 million. He played Dave Buznick, a wimpy guy who cannot muster the courage to kiss his girlfriend or stand up for himself at work. When he is mistakenly accused of assaulting an airline flight attendant, Dave is ordered to undergo anger management counseling in order to stay out of jail. He winds up working with a radical therapist (played by Jack Nicholson) whose unconventional methods make Dave truly angry. "Every Sandler movie is a course in anger management: in the care and feeding of rage, first suppressed, then geysering into an explosion of smashed crockery and punched-out supporting players," Richard Corliss noted in *Time*. "[But] even a longtime Adamphobe has to

*Sandler and Barrymore in a scene from the romantic comedy* 50 First Dates.

admit that Sandler is an agreeable presence here, and that the film . . . should make audiences happy."

In 2004 Sandler once again teamed up with Drew Barrymore in the romantic comedy *50 First Dates.* He played Henry Roth, a ladies' man who falls in love with a woman (Barrymore) who has no short-term memory. Roth wins her over one day, only to have her forget him by the next. Audiences flocked to see the movie, helping it to earn $120 million. Critical response was much more positive than for earlier films, and reviewers generally found it silly and sweet. "Sandler, confronted with a girl who can't remember him, is forced to become the ultimate romantic, a man who woos with every breath," Gleiberman noted in *Entertainment Weekly.* "The movie is sort of an experiment for Sandler," Roger Ebert wrote in the *Bergen Country Record.* "He reveals the warm side of his personality and leaves behind the hostility, anger, and gross-out humor. To be sure, there's projectile vomiting on a vast scale in an opening scene, but it's performed by a walrus, not one of the human characters. . . . This is a kinder and gentler Sandler." That view was echoed in the *Atlanta Journal-Constitution* by Eleanor Ringel Gillespie. "*50 First Dates* is an almost perfect Valentine's movie. Like the stars' last collaboration, *The Wedding Singer*, it's charmingly romantic and funny (think chick flick). And like so many of Sandler's lowest-common-denominator comedies, it's suffused with slapstick and gross-out gags (think very guy Sandler fan). *50 First Dates* comes down to chemistry. And who would have ever guessed the goofy little girl from *E.T.—The Extra-Terrestrial* and the goofy guy from *Billy Madison* could strike such delicious sparks."

Later in 2004, Sandler took on another serious role in *Spanglish*, directed by James L. Brooks. He played John Clasky, a successful Los Angeles chef struggling to raise two children with his neurotic wife (Tea Leoni). They hire a Mexican housekeeper (Paz Vega), who cannot speak English, a decision that ends up transforming their marriage and their family. Critics generally found that the story lacked focus, but they praised the actors' performances.

In 2005 Sandler appeared in *The Longest Yard*, a remake of a popular 1974 prison movie that starred Burt Reynolds. Sandler played a washed-up professional football player who gets sent to prison for smashing up his rich girlfriend's car. While there, he puts together a ragtag team of inmates to face the guards in a football game. "Led by Adam Sandler, a surprisingly effective quarterback for the convicts, the new version takes its audience on a fast-paced joyride of adult humor and body-slamming action," Rick Cantu wrote in the *Austin American-Statesman*. "With so much comedy provided by other characters, Sandler opts for a mature approach not often seen in his films. He absorbs punishment from sadistic guards and is roughed up by [former Dallas Cowboys wide receiver Michael Irvin] in a one-on-one game of basketball. It's all part of a skillful blend of action and comic relief, a remake that scores big."

> "
>
> "**50 First Dates** *is an almost perfect Valentine's movie," wrote critic Eleanor Ringel Gillespie. "Who would have ever guessed the goofy little girl from* E.T.—The Extra-Terrestrial *and the goofy guy from* Billy Madison *could strike such delicious sparks."*
>
> "

## Public Opinion

In addition to starring in movies, Sandler runs his own film-production company, Happy Madison Productions. The staff of his company, known as Team Sandler, consists mainly of his good friends from college. "Making a movie is a long process," he noted. "I want to be around people I can have fun with." Sandler exercises a great deal of creative control over his own movies—writing, producing, and choosing the director and supporting cast for many of them. "He's in charge of every detail of his comedy," said Henry Winkler, his co-star in *The Waterboy.* "He hears it in his head and guides whatever scene, whether he is in it or not, to his vision." Sandler also develops scripts for other comedians through Happy Madison Productions. The company has produced several movies for Rob Schneider, for instance, including *Deuce Bigalow: Male Gigolo* and *The Hot Chick.*

While Sandler is one of Hollywood's biggest stars and earns more than $20 million per picture, he is also very unpopular among some segments of the movie-going public, who find his acting wooden and his humor juvenile. Just as there are people who will go to see any Sandler movie, there are others who refuse to see any movie with him in it. "Just as the population is split between Republicans and Democrats, Coke and Pepsi drinkers, and SUV lovers and haters, so is it apparently divided over the appeal of Adam Sandler," Todd McCarthy explained in *Variety.*

—— " ——

*"He's a genius," said Amy Pascal, vice chairman of Sony Pictures. "He understands something none of the rest of us do—what makes people laugh, and what touches people's hearts."*

—— " ——

Film critics may dismiss Sandler's work, but audiences still flock to theaters whenever he releases a new movie. They know what they will get from the star, and they know that it will be entertaining. "It's unfair to put Adam's comedies into the larger world of film," said "Saturday Night Live" creator Lorne Michaels. "It is like comparing candy to the whole world of food. Everyone knows what a Snickers is and why you like it. To deconstruct it, to point out that it only has peanuts and chocolate, is to take all the fun out of eating it."

Given the remarkable success of his films, it is clear that Sandler has millions of dedicated fans who enjoy his silly humor, crazy antics, and typical storylines about an unlikely hero who manages to prevail despite himself. "There's just something really safe and likeable about seeing this guy up there," said comedian David Spade. "Even if you're only five years old, you poke your friend and say, 'At least I'm not as dumb as that idiot!'"

Sandler may play dumb characters in his movies. But within Hollywood, he receives a great deal of respect for his ability to understand his audience and fill the seats of movie theaters. "He's a genius," said Amy Pascal, vice chairman of Sony Pictures. "He understands something none of the rest of us do—what makes people laugh, and what touches people's hearts."

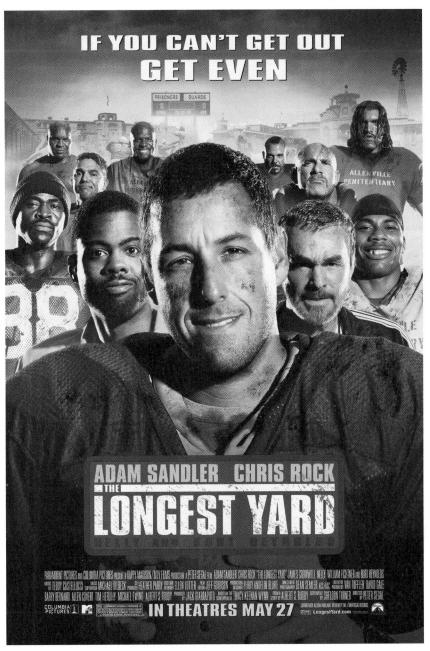

*Sandler teamed up with Chris Rock in* The Longest Yard.

## MARRIAGE AND FAMILY

Sandler married actress-model Jackie Titone on June 22, 2003. The wedding took place at sunset on a friend's oceanfront estate in Malibu, California. The otherwise traditional Jewish ceremony included Sandler's two bulldogs, Meatball and Matzoball, who wore tuxedos and carried the couple's wedding rings. "Jackie's the finest woman I've ever met," he stated. "She's got it all—brains, looks, a sense of humor, and most unbelievable of all, she likes me for me."

## SELECTED CREDITS

### Films

*Shakes the Clown*, 1991
*The Coneheads*, 1993
*Airheads*, 1994
*Billy Madison*, 1995 (also screenwriter)
*Happy Gilmore*, 1996 (also screenwriter)
*Bulletproof*, 1996
*The Wedding Singer*, 1998
*The Waterboy*, 1998 (also screenwriter)
*Big Daddy*, 1999 (also screenwriter)
*Little Nicky*, 2000 (also screenwriter)
*Punch-Drunk Love*, 2002
*Eight Crazy Nights*, 2002 (also screenwriter)
*Mr. Deeds*, 2002
*Anger Management*, 2003
*50 First Dates*, 2004
*Spanglish*, 2004
*The Longest Yard*, 2005

### Television

"Saturday Night Live," 1990-95

### Recordings

*They're All Gonna Laugh at You!*, 1993
*What the Hell Happened to Me?*, 1996
*What's Your Name?*, 1997
*The Wedding Singer: Original Motion Picture Soundtrack*, 1998
*Stan and Judy's Kid*, 1999
*Shhh . . . Don't Tell*, 2004

## HONORS AND AWARDS

MTV Movie Awards: 1996, for best fight in *Happy Gilmore* (with Bob Barker); 1998, for best kiss in *The Wedding Singer* (with Drew Barrymore); 1999, for best comedic performance in *The Waterboy*; 2000, for best comedic performance in *Big Daddy*; 2004, for best on-screen team in *50 First Dates* (with Drew Barrymore)

Blockbuster Entertainment Awards: 1999, for favorite actor/comedy in *The Wedding Singer* and *The Waterboy*; 2000, for favorite actor/comedy in *Big Daddy*

Kids' Choice Award as Favorite Actor: 1999, for *The Waterboy* and *The Wedding Singer*; 2000, for *Big Daddy*; 2003, for *Mr. Deeds*; 2005, for *50 First Dates*

People's Choice Awards: 2000, for favorite movie star/comedy; 2005, for favorite on-screen chemistry in *50 First Dates* (with Drew Barrymore)

Teen Choice Award as Best Comedian: 2001, 2002, 2004, 2005

## FURTHER READING

### Books

*Contemporary Musicians*, Vol. 19, 1997
Crawford, Bill. *Adam Sandler: America's Comedian*, 2000
Epstein, Dwayne. *People in the News: Adam Sandler*, 2004
*Newsmakers*, Issue 2, 1999
Seidman, David. *Adam Sandler*, 2001

### Periodicals

*Biography*, Apr. 2003, p.16
*Current Biography Yearbook*, 1998
*Entertainment Weekly*, Feb. 17, 1995, p.26; June 18, 1999, p.24; Oct. 18, 2002, p.87; Apr. 18, 2003, p.44; June 3, 2005, p.60
*Interview*, Dec. 1994, p.104
*Los Angeles Times*, Nov. 5, 2000, Calendar, p.8
*People*, Nov. 30, 1998, p.73
*Premiere*, Dec. 2004/Jan. 2005, p.110
*Time*, Nov. 23, 1998, p.102; Oct. 21, 2002, p.70
*USA Today*, Apr. 8, 1994, p.D5; Feb. 13, 1998, p.D18
*Washington Post*, Nov. 13, 1998, p.D1

### Online Databases

*Biography Resource Center Online*, 2005, articles from *Contemporary Authors Online*, 2003, and *Contemporary Musicians*, 1997

## ADDRESS

Adam Sandler
Happy Madison Productions, Inc.
10202 West Washington Blvd.
Culver City, CA 90232

## WORLD WIDE WEB SITE

http://www.adamsandler.com

## Jon Stewart 1962-
American Comedian and Actor
Host of "The Daily Show with Jon Stewart"

### BIRTH

Jonathan Stewart (some sources say "Stuart") Leibowitz was born on November 28, 1962, in Lawrence, New Jersey. He shortened his name to Jon Stewart in the mid-1980s, when he became a comedian. His father, Donald Leibowitz, was a physicist who worked for RCA. His mother, Marian, worked as an educational consultant and special-education teacher. He has one older brother, Larry.

## YOUTH

Even as a youngster, Stewart enjoyed making people laugh. But he admits that his constant joking probably got a little tiresome for those around him. "Some people can paint," he said. "I can't. Some people can sing. I can't. Some people make a joke of everything. I've done that since I was four or five years old. I don't remember a time when people didn't think I was a wiseass. I hope I've gotten more artful over time, because when I was younger, I was just obnoxious."

——— " ———

*"Some people can paint,"
Stewart said. "I can't.
Some people can sing.
I can't. Some people make
a joke of everything.
I've done that since
I was four or five years old.
I don't remember a time
when people didn't think
I was a wiseass. I hope
I've gotten more artful over
time, because
when I was younger,
I was just obnoxious."*

——— " ———

Stewart grew up in one of the few Jewish families in his neighborhood. His background often made him the target of name-calling and bullying. "They will find what is unique about you and destroy you for it," he observed. "So if you're Jewish and most people aren't, OK, let's go with that. But it just as easily could have been because I was short."

When Stewart was still a pre-teen, he was stunned when his parents informed him that they were getting a divorce. The situation became even more painful when his father made little effort to maintain a relationship with his sons afterward. From that point forward, Stewart was raised by his mother, whom he has described as "passionate about education and current events." Her passion about these issues was a big factor in his own evolving interest in politics and current affairs.

Despite his difficult adolescence, Stewart expresses great affection for his home state of New Jersey. "There are a lot of jokes about Jersey, but it really is a great place," he said. "It's a very diverse state. It's very diverse ethnically, religiously. There's different food, culture. To put it in perspective, Jersey is the perfect scarecrow. People see the turnpike and think, 'Oh, what a mess.' But five minutes from there, you'll find a great lake or great scenery. I like that people think it's a mess, then there's less people there and it's better for me."

## EDUCATION

Stewart attended public schools in Lawrence. After graduating from high school around 1980, he enrolled at Virginia's College of William and

Mary. He promptly joined a fraternity, but he resigned his membership after six months. He felt disgusted by the group's hazing practices, and he refused to pretend to be friends with frat brothers he did not even like. Stewart spent the next few years playing soccer, studying, and—by his own admission—partying too much. In 1984 he earned a bachelor's degree in psychology, then promptly returned to New Jersey. "I had no idea what I was doing [at college]," he admitted. "And then I got out and I still had no idea."

## FIRST JOBS

Stewart spent the next couple years moving from job to job, trying to find his place in the world. He staged puppet shows for disabled kids, worked as a contract administrator for a local college,

*Stewart got his start doing stand-up routines at various comedy clubs.*

conducted field research for a state study on encephalitis, and worked as a bartender. He enjoyed this carefree lifestyle on a day-to-day basis, but after a while he became restless. "I started thinking, 'This is it for the next 70 years?'" he recalled. "So I told my mom I was going to New York to do comedy. I never discussed it with the—what's the other one called?—dad."

Stewart landed in New York City in 1986. Looking back, he expressed pride in his decision to leave his safe existence behind and take a chance. "I might have become a bitter guy at the end of the bar, complaining about how I could've been somebody," he said. "But I sold my car and moved up to New York with no job because I wanted something different. I yearned, and I went for it."

## CAREER HIGHLIGHTS

### Diving into Stand-Up Comedy

Stewart found work in New York City as a bartender, then set about trying to establish himself in the ultra-competitive world of stand-up comedy.

One of the first things he did was to drop his last name and introduce himself as "Jon Stewart." After achieving stardom, Stewart said that he took this step because comedy club emcees and owners kept mispronouncing and misspelling his family name. But he has also hinted that he dropped the Leibowitz name in part because of his nonexistent relationship with his father.

Stewart endured some rough nights on stage during those early years. "The first night I ever went on stage, about three minutes into my stand-up act, some guy yelled, 'You suck.' And he hasn't stopped hounding me since," he joked. But with each passing night, Stewart became a little more sure of himself. "I never had any talent or affinity for any other artistic thing," he explained. "I went through a period of time where I said, 'I'm going to be a cartoonist. I'm going to be a novelist. I'm going to be a trumpet player.' A few weeks into each, it became apparent that it was not my calling. When I was on stage, the clouds didn't part and someone didn't call from above, 'Yes, you are a comedian,' but it was something I felt comfortable with."

> ———— " ————
>
> *"It was grueling and hilarious," Stewart said of his early stand-up days. "I remember walking home at three in the morning going, If it doesn't get any better than this, it's still better than I ever thought it'd be."*
>
> ———— " ————

By the late 1980s Stewart was known as one of the funniest comics in the city. Although he did not focus on the political humor that later became his ticket to fame, his act was full of wry and cutting observations about human nature and the American way of life. "It was grueling and hilarious," he said of his early stand-up days. "I remember walking home at three in the morning going, If it doesn't get any better than this, it's still better than I ever thought it'd be." He also was popular with other comedians, even though they were competing for spots in New York's top clubs. "I, like almost every other female in the comedy community, had a crush on him," recalled comedian Janeane Garofalo. "He's just one of those guys everybody likes."

Stewart's comic skills eventually attracted attention from promoters and entertainment executives across the country. He was invited to appear on several HBO comedy specials and on "Late Night with David Letterman." In the early 1990s he was selected to host "Short Attention Span Theater" on the Comedy Channel (now Comedy Central). From there he moved on to MTV, where in 1993 he was given his own half-hour talk show. When "The Jon Stewart Show" was canceled one year later, Paramount

*Stewart in his office.*

Studios promptly approached him about doing a syndicated one-hour talk show.

This show, also called "The Jon Stewart Show," won praise from a number of critics. They described Stewart's casual, conversational approach as a refreshing change of pace from the heavily scripted shows airing elsewhere on late-night TV. "[Stewart] seems like Letterman's younger, hipper brother," declared *People*.

Stewart's show struggled to find an audience, though. In addition, the comedian found that he was no longer having fun. "About four months into it, I thought, Wow, this unbelievable opportunity will be taken away from me, and when someone asks, Did you even enjoy it? I'm going to say no." Years later, Stewart described the show "as a watershed, and I don't mean comedically. I mean emotionally. I was playing scared. I was playing not to lose."

## Joining "The Daily Show"

In 1995 "The Jon Stewart Show" was cancelled after months of poor ratings and mixed critical reviews. The cancellation did not derail Stewart's career, though. Instead, he kept busy on a variety of cable television shows (including a recurring role on HBO's popular "Larry Sanders Show"). He also took supporting roles in a handful of films. He even wrote a book called *Naked Pictures of Famous People,* a 1998 collection of essays that took comic aim at everyone from Adolf Hitler to Martha Stewart.

In 1998 Stewart received a phone call from Comedy Central executives, who had been trying to get the comedian back on the network for several years. They asked him if he wanted to take over as host of "The Daily Show" in place of Craig Kilborn, who was leaving for another late night program. Stewart quickly accepted the offer, and in January 1999 he stepped on stage for the first time as host of "The Daily Show with Jon Stewart."

During Kilborn's years as host, the show's humor had focused on celebrities and weird news stories, and many of the jokes had a malicious edge to them. It did not take long for Stewart to decide that the show needed to change its tone and focus. "It was a conscious decision to move to relevance—to make the show something people care about," he said. "I did what I wanted to do, with like-minded people who'd bring passion, competence, and creativity to it."

Stewart freely admits that some members of the staff resisted the show's increasing focus on politics, current events, and the news media. In fact, a number of the writers continued to churn out mean-spirited material targeting ordinary Americans and harmless celebrities who found themselves in the news. "I can't tell you my first year here was particularly pleasant," he said. "I can't say there weren't days of knock-down, drag-'em-out yelling." But these writers gradually drifted away, and they were replaced by people who felt excited about the prospect of turning their comic ammunition on leading politicians and journalists.

By 2000 the content of "The Daily Show with Jon Stewart" was much more to Stewart's liking. Assisted by a group of fake news correspondents, Stewart offered audiences a nightly dose of comic news coverage that seemed to become more clever and insightful with each broadcast. The show's coverage of the 2000 presidential election, which it dubbed "Indecision 2000," was particularly funny and perceptive. These broadcasts, which relentlessly poked fun at the campaigns of both Republican nominee George W. Bush and Democratic nominee Al Gore, brought thousands of new viewers to the show.

### Becoming a "Fake News" Phenomenon

Over the next few years, Stewart and his colleagues perfected their fake-news act. Blending Stewart's anchorman monologues with fake feature stories and real interviews with politicians, journalists, and celebrities, the show's trademark mix of humorous political commentary attracted bigger audiences and earned greater critical praise with each passing month. By

*Stewart on the set of "The Daily Show."*

2001 *Esquire* magazine was describing "The Daily Show" as "the smartest, most innovative show on TV."

Reviewers agreed that Stewart was the glue that kept the show together. "Stewart's on-air persona is that of the outraged individual who, comparing official pronouncements with his own basic common sense, simply cannot believe what he—and all of us—are expected to swallow," wrote Susan J. Douglas in *The Nation*. According to *Rolling Stone* writer John Calapinto, this outrage is fed not only by Stewart's desire to get laughs, but also by his own take on world events. "Two minutes in Stewart's company shows you that he's scary smart," wrote Calapinto. "Stewart actually thinks about stuff. Serious stuff, and thinks about it critically and deeply."

By 2003 Stewart and his show had become a genuine force in American politics. "You simply can't understand American politics in the new millennium without 'The Daily Show,'" declared journalist Bill Moyers. With this in mind, in September 2003 U.S. Senator John Edwards decided to announce his candidacy for the 2004 Democratic presidential nomination on Stewart's show. Stewart responded by joking that the announcement did not count because it came on a fake news show.

Stewart downplayed his show's growing influence, insisting that he and the other writers and performers were just having fun. "There's a difference between making a point and having an agenda," he said. "We don't have an agenda to change the political system. We have a more selfish agenda, to entertain ourselves. We feel a frustration with the way politics are handled and the way politics are handled within the media."

## Creating Controversy on "Crossfire"

Despite Stewart's protests, Washington-based politicians and journalists agree that his show has become quite influential. This influence became clearer in 2004, when Stewart appeared on CNN's "Crossfire," a program in which liberal and conservative political analysts argue over the issues of the day. "Crossfire" hosts Paul Begala and Tucker Carlson clearly expected the interview with Stewart to consist of little more than light-hearted joking. Instead, Stewart used his appearance to raise concerns about the media in general and "Crossfire" in particular. Stewart criticized the program as "partisan hackery" that did not make a serious attempt to examine important issues. Carlson angrily told the comedian to tell some jokes, but Stewart continued to condemn "Crossfire" and similar news shows.

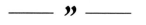

*"There's a difference between making a point and having an agenda," Stewart said. "We don't have an agenda to change the political system. We have a more selfish agenda, to entertain ourselves. We feel a frustration with the way politics are handled and the way politics are handled within the media."*

"The reason everyone on 'Crossfire' freaked out is that I didn't play the role I was supposed to play," Stewart later said. "I was expected to do some funny jokes, then go have a beer with everyone. By stepping outside of my role, I stunned them. Imagine going on 'Crossfire' and expressing an opinion that causes a problem. Apparently the only people you cannot put in the crossfire are the hosts of 'Crossfire.'... What I ultimately said was, 'Tomorrow I'll go back to being funny, and you guys will still blow.'... It was as if they thought I was suddenly taking myself too seriously. What do you think 'The Daily Show' is about? Just because we're comedic doesn't mean we don't care about this stuff. We do."

A few months later CNN announced the cancellation of "Crossfire." At that time, the network president, Jonathan Klein, admitted that Stewart's comments had been on target. "It's time for us to do a better job of informing our audience in an engaging way, as opposed to head-butting and screaming," he said.

**THE DAILY SHOW WITH JON STEWART PRESENTS**

# AMERICA

(THE BOOK)
★ ★ ★

**A Citizen's Guide to Democracy Inaction**

**With a Foreword by Thomas Jefferson**

### Writing *America (The Book)*

By the end of 2004 "The Daily Show" and its host had won numerous awards, including several Emmy and Peabody awards. The program also attracted more than a million viewers every night—triple the number of viewers it had when Kilborn was the host. In addition, research studies have indicated that people who watch the show are better informed about current events and American politics than people who rely on other news sources. "We don't make things up," explained Stewart. "We just distill it to, hopefully, its most humorous nugget. And in that sense it seems faked and skewed just because we don't have to be subjective or pretend to be objective. We can just put it out there."

Stewart and his fellow "Daily Show" writers have also branched out into writing books. In late 2004 they released *America (The Book): A Citizen's Guide to Democracy Inaction.* Organized like a weird textbook, it uses biting humor to comment on the country's history and the current state of its government institutions and news media. An immediate bestseller, it was widely praised by reviewers. *People* called it "a hilarious book with a distinct liberal bias.... Rude, crude, and utterly delightful." *Fortune*'s Brian O'Keefe described it as "truly laugh-out-loud funny. How do I know? When it first arrived on my desk, I opened it to a random page and immediately laughed out loud."

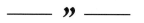

*"We don't make things up,"* Stewart explained. *"We just distill it to, hopefully, its most humorous nugget. And in that sense it seems faked and skewed just because we don't have to be subjective or pretend to be objective. We can just put it out there."*

*America (The Book)* made such a huge splash that *Publishers Weekly* named it the book of the year for 2004. "Beneath the eye-catching and at times goofy graphics, the dirty jokes and the playful ingenuousness, shines a serious critique of the two-party system, the corporations that finance it, and the 'spineless cowards in the press' who 'aggressively print allegation and rumor independent of accuracy or fairness,'" declared the magazine.

Meanwhile, Stewart and his "Daily Show" colleagues continue to make fun of American politicians and political parties in all sorts of clever ways. "The Daily Show" holds both Democrats and Republicans up for ridicule, but most observers agree that it takes special delight in attacking the Bush administration. Stewart admits that he thinks Bush is a poor president who often misleads the American people. But he insists that his show is not a public relations arm of the rival Democratic Party, and he points out numerous occasions when he and his colleagues have made Democratic lawmakers look bad.

In many ways, though, the biggest target of "The Daily Show" is the American news media. In Stewart's view, most American news organizations no longer make much of an effort to force politicians to tell the truth or behave ethically. "Politicians are doing what politicians do," Stewart said. "I liken it to when you go to the zoo, and the monkeys are sitting in there ... throwing their s—. And you just gotta go, 'Well, they're monkeys.' But you can yell at the media and go, 'You know, your job is to tell them when they're being bad monkeys.' ... The TV networks have an opportunity to bring noise or clarity. So much of what the government and corporations do is bring noise because they don't welcome scrutiny. They don't necessarily want you to know what they're up to. So if you're working in a medium that has an opportunity to bring clarity and you instead choose to create more distraction, that's theater—which is what these news channels have become."

In 2004 "Daily Show" fans rejoiced when Stewart signed a new contract that will keep him behind the anchor desk on the show through the 2008 presidential election. Stewart admits that he is happy with the agreement, which pays him about $2 million a year. But he insists that he will not stay on "The Daily Show" forever, because he has other projects he would like to pursue. "I want to breed a race of ninjas," he joked.

## MARRIAGE AND FAMILY

In 2000 Stewart married Tracy McShane, a veterinary technician, after a long courtship. They live in Manhattan with their son, Nathan Thomas. "We usually have a nice dinner, play with the dog, watch whatever's on, do a crossword puzzle together, and go to bed," Stewart said. "I hate to say it: I feel content. And driven at the same time. Hopefully, that's a combination that will work for a while."

## HOBBIES AND OTHER INTERESTS

Stewart enjoys reading on a wide range of subjects, including American history and current events. He is also a big sports fan.

## SELECTED CREDITS

### Television

"Short Attention Span Theater," 1991-92
"You Wrote It, You Watch It," 1992
"The Jon Stewart Show," 1993-95
"The Daily Show with Jon Stewart," 1999-

### Films

*Playing by Heart,* 1998
*The Faculty,* 1998
*Barenaked in America,* 1999
*Big Daddy,* 1999

*Jay and Silent Bob Strike Back,* 2001
*Death to Smoochie,* 2002

## Writings

*Naked Pictures of Famous People,* 1998
*America (The Book): A Citizen's Guide to Democracy Inaction,* 2004 (with
    the writers of "The Daily Show with Jon Stewart")

## HONORS AND AWARDS

George F. Peabody Award: 2001, for "Indecision 2000" coverage on "The
    Daily Show with Jon Stewart"; 2005, for "Indecision 2004" coverage on
    "The Daily Show with Jon Stewart"
Emmy Award: 2003 and 2004, for best writing for a comedy series, for
    "The Daily Show with Jon Stewart"; 2004, for best variety, musical, or
    comedy show, for "The Daily Show with Jon Stewart"
Book of the Year (*Publishers Weekly*): 2004, for *America (The Book)*
Best News and Information Program (Television Critics Association):
    2004, for "The Daily Show with Jon Stewart"
100 Most Influential People (*Time*): 2005

## FURTHER READING

### Books

*Authors and Artists for Young Adults,* Vol. 57, 2004
*Who's Who in America,* 2005

### Periodicals

*Cosmopolitan,* Jan. 1, 1999
*Current Biography Yearbook,* 2004
*Entertainment Weekly,* Oct. 31, 2003, p.30; Sep. 17, 2004, p.10
*Esquire,* July 2001, p.62
*Fortune,* Sep. 20, 2004, p.60
*Los Angeles Times,* Nov. 30, 1994, p.F1
*Nation,* May 5, 2003, p.24
*New York Times,* Mar. 13, 1994, Section 2, p.34; Oct. 3, 2004, Section 7,
    p.20
*New Yorker,* Feb. 11, 2002, p.28
*Newsweek,* July 31, 2000, p.60; Dec. 29, 2003, p.70
*O Magazine,* June 2005, p.186
*People,* Apr. 4, 1994, p.99; Dec. 27, 2004, p.63
*Publishers Weekly,* Sep. 28, 1998, p.73; Sep. 6, 2004, p.58; Dec. 6, 2004, p.31

*Rolling Stone,* Jan. 26, 1995, p.26; Oct. 28, 2004, p.58
*Washington Post,* Apr. 16, 1995, p.G8; May 2, 2002, p.C1; Oct. 23, 2004,
    p.A1

## Online Articles

http://www.cbsnews.com/stories
    (*CBS News,* "60 Minutes: Jon Stewart Roasts Real News,"
    Dec. 21, 2004)
http://www.pbs.org/now
    (*NOW with Bill Moyers,* "Bill Moyers Interviews Jon Stewart,"
    July 11, 2003)

## Online Databases

*Biography Resource Center Online,* 2005, articles from *Authors and
    Artists for Young Adults,* 2004, and *Contemporary Authors Online,*
    2004

## ADDRESS

Jon Stewart
"The Daily Show with Jon Stewart"
Comedy Central Viewer Services
1775 Broadway, 10th Floor
New York, NY 10019

## WORLD WIDE WEB SITE

http://www.comedycentral.com/shows/the_daily_show

## Joss Stone 1987-

British Soul Singer
Creator of the Popular Albums *The Soul Sessions* and
*Mind, Body, & Soul*

### BIRTH

Joss Stone was born as Joscelyn Eve Stoker on April 11, 1987,
in the town of Dover, Kent, England. She adopted her stage
name at 14, when she signed her first recording contract. Joss
was the third of four children born to Richard Stoker, who
ran a dried-fruit business, and Wendy Stoker, who managed
vacation cottages. She has an older brother, Daniel; an older
sister, Lucy; and a younger brother, Harry.

## YOUTH

Joss grew up in rural Devon, in the English countryside. Although her parents were not musical, they greatly enjoyed listening to music and exposed their children to a range of musical styles. Her father tended to favor rock and roll, and he was an avid fan of the Beatles. Her mother leaned more toward folk and soul music, and her favorites included Melissa Etheridge and the Motown sound. "My parents used to play a lot of music around the house," she recalled. "Some of it was soul, some of it wasn't."

Thanks to her parents' influence, Joss enjoyed all sorts of music as a girl. Her interest turned toward soul at the age of 12, when she heard a greatest hits album by Aretha Franklin, the Motown recording artist known as the "Queen of Soul." "In a way, soul found me," she explained. "I kind of clicked into soul more than anything else because of the vocals. You've got to have good vocals to sing soul music." Joss always liked to sing, but she never took any formal voice lessons. "I learned to sing by listening to Aretha Franklin," she noted. "She was my teacher."

> **"**
>
> *"In a way, soul found me," Stone explained. "I kind of clicked into soul more than anything else because of the vocals. You've got to have good vocals to sing soul music."*
>
> **"**

When Joss was 13, she overcame her natural shyness to audition for "Star for a Night," a talent program that was televised in England by the BBC (the U.S. version of the show is "American Idol"). She earned a spot on the show by singing Aretha Franklin's soul classic "(You Make Me Feel Like a) Natural Woman" at the audition. Most of the teenagers who performed on the program sang pop songs in the manner of Britney Spears, and members of the audience expected Joss to follow suit. Instead, she blew away the competition by turning in a mature, soulful performance of Donna Summer's "On the Radio."

Joss's brilliant performance on "Star for a Night" earned her a contract with a talent agent. A few months later, she and her mother flew to New York City so that Joss could audition for Steve Greenberg, the head of S-Curve Records. Since Joss had not even prepared a "demo" tape yet, Greenberg downloaded some karaoke tracks from the Internet and asked her to sing along with such classics as "Midnight Train to Georgia" and "(Sittin' on the) Dock of the Bay." "When I first heard her sing, I really couldn't believe that this big, soulful, nuanced, precious, wonderful, knowing voice was coming out of this 14-year-old girl," Greenberg recalled. "I was half-convinced there was a hidden tape recorder some-where." He immediately signed her to a recording contract with S-Curve.

## EDUCATION

Joss attended the Uffculme Comprehensive School near Cullumpton, England. She struggled in school because she suffers from a mild form of dyslexia, a condition in which the brain mixes up the order and direction of letters and numbers. "Always, on my school report card, I'd get 'Must try harder,' or 'Joscelyn has a problem with remembering,'" she noted. Joss sang in the school choir and per-formed in some student plays. But she found academics so frustrating that she was desperate to quit school, and signing a record deal gave her that opportunity. She ended her education in 2002, at the age of 15, after taking the necessary exams to earn a General Certificate of Secondary Education (GCSE), the equivalent of an Ameri-can high school diploma.

> "
>
> "When I first heard her sing, I really couldn't believe that this big, soulful, nuanced, precious, wonderful, knowing voice was coming out of this 14-year-old girl," recalled Steve Greenberg, the head of S-Curve Records. "I was half-convinced there was a hidden tape recorder somewhere."
>
> "

## CAREER HIGHLIGHTS

### Working on *The Soul Sessions*

After signing with S-Curve Records, Stone was eager to begin working on an album. She expected to follow the usual process for new artists: write some songs, then put together a band and record them. But Greenberg had another idea. He felt that the best way to showcase Stone's unique voice would be to have her team up with well-known musicians and record some soul classics of the 1970s. "He had the idea of doing an EP [extended play] with these soul legends," Stone recalled. "Then it turned into this whole album thing."

Greenberg sent Stone to Miami, Florida, to work with Betty Wright, a Grammy Award–winning gospel and soul singer and record producer. Like Stone, Wright had launched her singing career during her teen years, and she went on to record a number of hit songs during the 1970s. Wright was pleased to work with the young British singer, whose voice she described as "a gift from heaven." "She's really like an oxymoron—she's young but she's old," Wright said of Stone. "She could go pop but she's definitely soulful. She has a soulful base." Wright became a mentor to Stone and pushed her to develop her talents. "She has a pair of drumsticks that she carries around with her—all the time," Stone noted. "So every time I'd do something wrong, she'd get her sticks out and threaten me with them. It's really funny. She's crazy like that."

Wright used her connections in the music industry to assemble a top-notch band for Stone's album. It featured legendary soul musicians from the 1960s and 1970s, like guitarist Willie "Little

*Stone with her mentor and collaborator, Betty Wright.*

Beaver" Hale and pianist Benny Latimore. Wright and Stone then selected vintage soul and R&B songs that had enjoyed some success in their time, but had not become top hits, and therefore might seem new to today's audiences. "I didn't write those songs, but I can relate to every one of them," Stone stated. "It's soul music. I have to feel it, in order to sing it with a little bit of soul." Finally, Wright arranged for Stone to perform duets with such well-known artists as Mick Jagger, Donna Summer, Chaka Khan, and Melissa Etheridge.

Stone released the result of these efforts, an album of covers entitled *The Soul Sessions*, in 2003. The album featured 70 musicians, yet it was recorded in only four days. "It was weird because they've worked with so many great, great singers," she recalled of the recording sessions. "I kind of walked in, just like this little girl, and started singing. I felt a bit weird about the whole thing because, 'Should I be here?' But it was cool because they made me feel really comfortable."

Executives at S-Curve Records did not expect *The Soul Sessions* to be a major release. They only hoped that its songs would receive some radio airplay in order to generate interest in the other album Stone was working on, which would feature her own songs. To the surprise of many, however, *The Soul Sessions* created a sensation. It sold over two million copies and appeared on *Billboard* magazine's list of the Top 40 albums in the United States. One of the most popular singles was "Fell in Love with a Boy," a remake of the White Stripes' song "Fell in Love with a Girl." The video for

the song debuted on MTV in early 2004, bringing Stone's music to a wider audience.

### Releasing *Mind, Body, & Soul*

The success of *The Soul Sessions* brought Stone a great deal of public attention. The 16-year-old was the subject of numerous interviews, and she appeared as a guest on many talk and variety shows, including "The Oprah Winfrey Show" and "The Tonight Show with Jay Leno." For Stone, one of the best things about her newfound fame was getting the opportunity to meet some of her musical inspirations. She enjoyed performing a duet with Smokey Robinson on the "Motown Records 45th Anniversary" television special, for instance, and she was thrilled to sing with Gladys Knight on "VH1 Divas." "To meet, let alone sing, with Gladys," she enthused. "The power and control in that voice! I learnt so much that day, just from being in her presence." Stone also became the opening act for a concert tour by the rock star Sting.

In the meantime, Stone continued working on what she considered her "real debut album," *Mind, Body, & Soul.* Unlike *The Soul Sessions*, which consists exclusively of cover versions of previously recorded songs, Stone wrote or co-wrote 80 percent of the material for this album. As a result, it features a more funky, R&B-inspired sound than her earlier record.

*Mind, Body, & Soul* was released in September 2004 to rave reviews. Renee Graham of the *Boston Globe* called it "one of the year's best albums" and said that "Stone again proves she has talent to burn and soul to spare." Many reviewers commented on Stone's powerful voice and its ability to convey a range of emotions. *Interview* magazine critic Dimitri Ehrlich said that her voice "can sting like aged bourbon or melt like strap molasses." "She can croon it sad, deep and throaty, belt it out juke-joint style, or get down and funky for the bump and grind crowd," Lorraine Ali added in *Newsweek*. "And most of all, the girl has attitude."

*Mind, Body, & Soul* debuted at the top of the album charts in the United Kingdom, making Stone the youngest female artist to accomplish this feat.

It also reached No. 11 on the *Billboard* album charts in the United States and was certified platinum, meaning that it sold over one million copies. Hit singles from the album included "Right to be Wrong" and "You Had Me." Another song, "Wicked Time," featuring Mick Jagger, appeared on the soundtrack of the 2004 movie *Alfie*.

Riding the success of her two albums, Stone won two British music industry awards in 2005, for Best British Female Artist and Best Urban Act. She was also nominated for three Grammy Awards that year, for Best New Artist, Best Pop Vocal Album, Best Female Pop Vocal Performance. Although Stone did not win a Grammy, she turned in one of the best performances of the televised award special. She teamed with folk singer Melissa Etheridge to sing "Cry Baby/ Piece of My Heart," a tribute to the late singer Janis Joplin. Their duet was later released as a single that appeared in *Billboard*'s Top 40.

### Showcasing Her Natural Talent

Throughout Stone's rise to stardom, the media has often made mention of the fact that she is not a "typical" soul singer. But Stone rejects this premise. "Everyone keeps saying it's surprising that I sing like a 50-year-old black woman. [But] that comment makes no sense to me. Music doesn't look like anything," she stated. "People need to get over it. My whole point is, people shouldn't listen with their eyes.... Soul comes from everywhere: black, white, pink, purple, it doesn't matter."

*"Everyone keeps saying it's surprising that I sing like a 50-year-old black woman. [But] that comment makes no sense to me. Music doesn't look like anything," Stone stated. "People need to get over it. My whole point is, people shouldn't listen with their eyes. . . . Soul comes from everywhere: black, white, pink, purple, it doesn't matter."*

At the start of her career, Stone considered singing pop songs like so many of her peers. But she soon realized that soul music allowed her to better express her interests and utilize her talent. "Pop music doesn't annoy me, I just don't want to do it," she explained. Stone also differentiates herself from other teenaged singing sensations in her usual attire— she prefers jeans and hoodie sweatshirts to the short skirts and tight tops usually seen on today's pop stars. Stone's habit of performing in bare feet has generated rumors about her wanting to be "closer to the earth," but she claims that "the real reason is that I don't want to fall over" on stage wearing high-heeled shoes.

Stone has experienced some problems with her vocal cords. After a hectic period of touring in 2004, she developed nodules due to strain. "I do worry my voice is going to stop working one day," she admitted. "I wish certain people would realize that I need time off occasionally and that if I keep on at this pace it could really damage me." Still, Stone remained busy in 2005. She performed at the London Live 8 charity concert, which raised money to help eliminate poverty worldwide. She also opened a series of concerts for the Rolling Stones. Seeking to expand her musical horizons, Stone collaborated with Dave Grohl of the Foo Fighters to write a rock song. She also signed a contract to become the new commercial spokesperson for The Gap clothing stores, taking the place of actress Sarah Jessica Parker in print and television advertisements.

With her mature music and constant media presence, it seems hard to believe that Stone is still a teenager. "People say I'm an old soul," she acknowledged. "I guess you could say I'm wise beyond my years, but I don't know where the wisdom comes from. I just trust my instincts."

## HOME AND FAMILY

Stone, who is single, lives in England. Her mother acts as her manager and travels with her during concert tours, personal appearances, and recording sessions. Stone bought a home of her own near Devon, England, shortly after she turned 18. She has a pet poodle named Dusty Springfield, after the British singer who was known as the "White Lady of Soul" in the 1960s and 1970s. "I'm fully aware that it's kind of Paris Hilton to carry around the little dog," Stone acknowledged. "But man, oh man! She is the cutest thing in the world."

## RECORDINGS

*The Soul Sessions*, 2003
*Mind, Body, & Soul*, 2004

## HONORS AND AWARDS

British Music Awards: 2005, for Best British Female Artist and
    Best Urban Act

## FURTHER READING

### Books

*Contemporary Musicians*, Vol. 52, 2005

### Periodicals

*Boston Globe*, Sep. 28, 2004, p.E1
*Daily Telegraph* (London), Sep. 18, 2004, p.4
*Entertainment Weekly*, June 24, 2005, p.108
*Interview*, Aug. 2004, p.98
*Newsweek*, Sep. 20, 2004, p.55
*Observer* (London), Jan. 19, 2004, p.18
*People Weekly*, Oct. 4, 2004, p.49; Nov. 8, 2004, p.115
*Teen People*, Dec. 2004, p.52
*Times* (London), Sep. 4, 2004, p.22
*Vogue*, Sep. 2004, p.582
*YM*, Oct. 2004, p.102

### Online Articles

http://www.mtv.com/news
    (MTV.com, "You Hear It First: Joss Stone," undated)

**Online Databases**

*Biography Resource Center Online*, 2005, article from
   *Contemporary Musicians*, 2005

Further information for this profile came from an interview with Stone
   that aired on National Public Radio on September 13, 2003.

## ADDRESS

Joss Stone
EMI USA
6255 West Sunset Blvd.
Hollywood, CA 90028

## WORLD WIDE WEB SITES

http://www.jossstone.co.uk
http://www.bbc.co.uk/devon/entertainment/music/index.shtml
http://www.bbc.co.uk/devon/entertainment/music/joss_stone/

## Brenda Villa 1980-
American Water Polo Player
Two-Time Olympic Medalist

### BIRTH

Brenda Villa (pronounced VEE-yah) was born on April 18, 1980, in East Los Angeles, California. Her parents, Ines and Rosario Villa, were both apparel workers. Brenda is the middle child in her family with an older brother Edgar, and a younger brother, Uriel.

### YOUTH

Shortly before Brenda was born, the Villas immigrated from their native Mexico to Commerce, California—a predominantly Latino neighborhood on the east side of Los Angeles. Throughout her childhood, the Villas lived across the street from the Commerce Aquatorium. This nationally renowned swim center, built in 1961, offered free pool access and swimming lessons to the local community. Over the years, the Commerce Aquatorium produced a number of Olympic swimmers. In the early 1970s the center started hosting water polo leagues.

The sport of water polo got its start in England during the 19th century. It is most similar to the British sport of rugby, except that it is played in the water. A game of water polo is divided into four periods of seven minutes each, but periods often last longer due to penalties and time-outs, so an average game lasts around 45 minutes. Water polo teams consist of seven players, including a goalkeeper. Each team tries to score goals by throwing the ball into the opponent's net. A team can only control the ball for a maximum of 35 seconds at a time, however, before it either scores a goal or turns over possession to the other team.

Water polo is a physically demanding sport. In addition to swimming back and forth across the pool, players must be able to throw a ball while remaining afloat and fending off opposing players. Games of water polo often involve rough play, with grabbing, kicking, scratching, and punching taking place between competitors. Penalties are handled like those in ice hockey, with the offending player sent to a penalty area for a certain amount of time, and the opposition allowed to continue with a player advantage.

By the mid-1980s, the Commerce Aquatorium had achieved recognition as one of the top water polo training grounds in the United States. Brenda first became interested in the sport at age six, when her brother Edgar joined a local boys' team. As soon as she saw her brother play, Brenda starting begging her mother to let her play, too. But Rosario Villa could not swim, and she feared for her little daughter's safety in a pool full of thrashing swimmers. After two years of hearing Brenda ask to try water polo, though, her mother finally gave in.

Since there were no girls' water polo teams at that time, Brenda joined a boys' team. Playing with the boys helped her become aggressive and mentally tough. "You have to anticipate more because the boys are quicker and stronger," she explained. "I mean, you could see there was a disadvantage when I was guarding a guy that was six-foot-two and 200 pounds and could, like, bench-press me. So I figured out how to take any advantage they had and equalize it or take it away from them."

Despite her obvious talent for the sport, Brenda endured both verbal and physical harassment as a girl playing on boys' teams. "I hear comments like, 'Why are you playing a man's sport?'" she acknowledged. "But I don't get mad. Instead of getting into arguments or fights with boys, you score goals on them." From the beginning of her water polo career, the one boy Brenda wanted to impress was her older brother. "He's not one to give out compliments," she noted. "Whenever I did something, I wanted his approval. It was a way to motivate myself."

## EDUCATION

Brenda attended Bell Gardens High School in Los Angeles. She played on the boys' water polo team because the school did not have a girls' team. During her freshman season in 1995, Brenda was her team's third-leading scorer with 44 goals. As a sophomore she scored 57 goals to help Bell Gardens win the California Division III High School Championship. Her brother Edgar, who was a senior that year, was named the Division III Player of the Year and went on to play water polo at Citrus College.

———— **"** ————

*"I hear comments like, 'Why are you playing a man's sport?'" Villa acknowledged. "But I don't get mad. Instead of getting into arguments or fights with boys, you score goals on them."*

———— **"** ————

As a junior in 1997 Brenda scored 48 goals to lead her high school team to a second consecutive state championship. During her senior year, *Water Polo* magazine named her as the top young female player in the world. Villa also made the All-California Interscholastic Federation Team three times during her high school career. By the time she graduated with honors in 1998, Villa was widely viewed as the top female water polo recruit in the country.

After considering a number of offers, Villa accepted an athletic scholarship to Stanford University. She decided to "red-shirt" the 1999 and 2000 collegiate seasons, meaning that she could practice with the team but not compete. She made this decision in order retain her college eligibility while also training for the 2000 Olympic Games. "When I was 17 [water polo] was announced as an Olympic sport," she recalled. "I could actually say that I was training for something." Villa started playing women's water polo for Stanford in 2001, and she remained the top player on the Cardinal team for the next two seasons. She graduated from Stanford with a bachelor's degree in political science in 2003.

## CAREER HIGHLIGHTS

### Earning a Silver Medal at the 2000 Olympics

When she was just 16 years old, Villa became a member of the U.S. National Women's Water Polo Team, which represents the country in international competitions like the Olympic Games. She was the first Hispanic woman ever to make the team. Villa played the position of "driver," which is an offensive position that involves passing or shooting the ball from the sides of the pool. Although she was shorter and stockier than most high-level water polo players, she was very well-rounded. "You look at her and you'd never think she's an Olympic athlete," U.S. Olympic Water Polo Coach Guy Baker acknowledged. "Brenda's one of our best swimmers, and she has tremendous endurance. She can go and go. The truth is, Brenda's just an athletic marvel." Villa particularly excelled as a playmaker—creating scoring chances for her team by either distributing the ball to open teammates or driving toward the goal herself.

> *"You look at her and you'd never think she's an Olympic athlete," acknowledged U.S. Olympic Water Polo coach Guy Baker. "Brenda's one of our best swimmers, and she has tremendous endurance. She can go and go. The truth is, Brenda's just an athletic marvel."*

For most of her high school years, Villa traveled to San Diego once a month for a three-day training camp with the national team. She also played in a number of major international competitions. She was the leading scorer on the U.S. team at the 1996 Women's World Cup, for instance, and she was the only high school player on the American team that competed in the 1998 Women's Water Polo World Championships.

After graduating from high school, Villa delayed the start of her college water polo career in order to concentrate on preparing for the 2000 Olympic Games in Sydney, Australia. The Sydney Games marked the debut of women's water polo as an Olympic sport. Men's water polo had been contested in the Olympics for more than a century, but the women's game was added only after many protests and a threatened lawsuit. Despite her youth, Villa played a critical role in earning the United States team a spot in the Olympic tournament, scoring the game-winning goal against Hungary in a "do or die" qualification game.

*Villa's strong swimming skills help her with underwater plays.*

In Sydney, the U.S. team made it through a tough pool to advance to the gold-medal match against the top-ranked Australian team. Villa scored the first goal of the game, but the Aussies came roaring back. With the American team trailing 3-2 near the end of the game, Villa scored the tying goal with 13.1 seconds left in the fourth period. It looked like the two teams would go to overtime, but then the referee called a controversial penalty on Villa. Australia, with a player advantage, ended up scoring the game-winning goal with just 1.3 seconds left on the clock. Australia thus captured the first-ever gold medal awarded in women's water polo, and Villa and her teammates were forced to settle for silver.

## Playing College Water Polo at Stanford University

After sitting out for two seasons, Villa finally began playing water polo for Stanford in 2001. She immediately proved to be worth the wait. Villa scored 69 goals that year to help lead her team to a 27-1 record. She scored in 25 games, and she scored two or more goals in 22 games, including a season-high six goals against the University of Southern California (USC).

Stanford advanced to the NCAA championship, where Villa's two goals were not quite enough to lift her team to victory. Stanford lost a heart-

*While attending Stanford University, Villa led her team to three consecutive NCAA championships.*

breaker to the University of California-Los Angeles (UCLA) by a score of 5-4. Villa won the prestigious NCAA Division I Player of the Year Award from the American Water Polo Coaches Association. She was also named a First Team All-American and Stanford's Female Athlete of the Year.

In 2002 Stanford had a perfect season, posting a 25-0 record and defeating UCLA for the national title. Villa led her team with 60 goals on the year, including five during the NCAA tournament. She was named NCAA Player of the Year and a First Team All-American for the second consecutive year. In addition, the Stanford Athletic Board honored her with the Block "S" Outstanding Female Sophomore Award. Finally, Villa received the Pete J. Cutino Award, which is presented annually to the top collegiate female water polo player in the nation by the Olympic Club.

In 2003 Stanford posted a 20-2 record and reached the national championship game for a third consecutive year. Once again, the Cardinal faced UCLA and lost a heartbreaker, 4-3. Villa scored 43 goals on the year to bring her career total to 172, which made her Stanford's all-time second-leading scorer. She earned NCAA Player of the Year and First Team All-American honors for the third straight year.

Stanford Coach John Tanner provided his views on why Villa was such a dominant collegiate player. "She has always had this incredible sense of the game, an almost unreal ability to anticipate what's going to happen," he explained. "She puts herself in a position where the ball can find her. She's able to see the game from a low angle in the water and she also seems to have a feel for what's going on as if she were standing above the play. That's extremely rare, a real gift. She has perspective to the point where it looks as if she was born to play water polo."

## Winning a Bronze Medal at the 2004 Olympics

Throughout her college water polo career, Villa continued playing internationally with the U.S. National Women's Water Polo Team. Shortly after competing in the 2001 NCAA Championships, for instance, Villa traveled to Greece, where she helped the U.S. team win the Thetis Cup tournament. She also played with the national team at the 2001 World Championships in Fukuoka, Japan, where the team placed fourth.

In 2002, during her college off-season, Villa helped lead the U.S. National Team to the Women's World Cup championship in Perth, Australia. The following year, she scored 13 goals to lead the American team to victory at the 2003 World Championships in Barcelona, Spain. Villa and her teammates became the first non-European team ever to be crowned world champions in women's water polo.

———— **"** ————

*"[She has] an almost unreal ability to anticipate what's going to happen," explained coach John Tanner. "She's able to see the game from a low angle in the water and she also seems to have a feel for what's going on as if she were standing above the play. That's extremely rare, a real gift. She has perspective to the point where it looks as if she was born to play water polo."*

———— **"** ————

The U.S. team's successful showing created high expectations for the 2004 Olympic Games in Athens, Greece. The highly regarded Americans had seven returning players from the silver-medal team of 2000. But they ended up playing in a tough bracket, which included the Eastern European powers Russia and Hungary. The U.S. team still managed to advance to the semifinals, where they suffered a heartbreaking loss to Italy, 6-5. The Americans had held a 4-2 advantage at one point, and Italy scored the winning goal with just two seconds left in the game.

*Villa with her 2004 Olympic teammates, proudly displaying their medals.*

The semifinal loss cost the American team a chance to play for the gold medal. (Italy went on to win the gold medal over Greece.) Instead, the U.S. team faced Australia to determine who would go home with the bronze. "We left Sydney with bittersweet memories [in 2000]," Villa recalled. "We didn't want to go from [Athens] without anything." The determined Americans came out strong and took a 4-0 lead after two periods, but the Aussies rallied to tie the score with just over five minutes remaining in the game. Luckily, Ellen Estes of the United States scored the game winner with 2:20 left to give her team the bronze. "We wanted to be on that podium," Villa said afterward. "We wanted gold, but at least we were on the podium getting something."

Villa was the leading scorer for the American team during the Olympic tournament, and she was named to the Olympic All-Star team. Coach Guy Baker praised Villa's contributions in Athens, describing her as the "quarterback" of the U.S. team. "Over the last six months, she's [been] one of the better players in the world," he stated. "She's stronger, she swims better and faster. Her vision's great and she creates opportunities." Villa agreed that her role had expanded since her first Olympic experience. "I'm probably better-rounded," she noted. "I kind of have a leadership role in the water. I sort of do whatever I see needs doing. I try to communicate a lot." While she was not the official team captain, Villa emerged as its vocal leader. "She's our voice. She's the energy," said Baker. "And that's great. We feed off that."

## Promoting Her Sport

Since the 2004 Olympics, Villa has divided her time between the U.S. National Team and Club Orizante in Catania, Italy. In her spare time, she returns to the Commerce Aquatorium, where she helps younger players develop their skills. Her younger brother, Uriel, is the latest member of the family to take up the sport of water polo at the facility. Villa is not sure yet whether she will try to compete in the 2008 Olympic Games in Beijing, China. She is considering going back to college for a graduate degree in public policy. "I'd like to go into some aspect of politics," she explained. "Not run for office or anything like that. But be one of those behind-the-scene people."

In 2005 *USA Today* listed Villa among its top Latina athletic role models, along with Olympic softball player Lisa Fernandez and professional golfer Lorena Ochoa. Given the small number of Hispanic players involved in water polo, Villa feels a responsibility to set an example. "I feel like water polo is a pretty expensive sport—it's not as accessible to train for as soccer or other Latin sports," she stated. "So I try to give back as much as they've given me."

> *"How many [young people] have had the opportunity to have traveled all over the world like I have?" Villa said. "The friendships I've built through playing the sport have been tremendous. What I like most about playing water polo is its tremendous competitiveness and also the camaraderie you have with your teammates."*

Villa says that she will always appreciate the opportunities that water polo gave her. "How many [young people] have had the opportunity to have traveled all over the world like I have?" she said. "The friendships I've built through playing the sport have been tremendous. What I like most about playing water polo is its tremendous competitiveness and also the camaraderie you have with your teammates." She hopes to influence young people to take up the sport as well. "I want little girls to grow up saying, 'I want to be a water polo player,'" she stated. "This sport has been so good to me, I feel I should return the favor."

## HOME AND FAMILY

Villa is single and lives in a studio apartment in Long Beach, California. She returns to Commerce often to visit family and friends.

## HOBBIES AND OTHER INTERESTS

In her "down time," Villa likes to relax by watching sports and reality shows on television. She also enjoys reading mystery novels.

## HONORS AND AWARDS

Best Young Female Player in the World (*Water Polo*): 1998
Olympic Women's Water Polo: 2000, silver medal; 2004, bronze medal
NCAA Division I Player of the Year (American Water Polo Coaches
    Association): 2001, 2002, 2003
NCAA Women's Water Polo First Team All-American: 2001, 2002, 2003
Pete J. Cutino Award (Olympic Club): 2002
NCAA Women's Water Polo National Championship: 2002, with
    Stanford University Cardinal
Women's Water Polo World Cup: 2002
Women's Water Polo World Championship: 2003

## FURTHER READING

### Books

Menard, Valerie. *Latinos at Work: Careers in Sports,* 2002

### Periodicals

*Boston Globe,* Aug. 27, 2004, p.E3
*Charlotte Observer,* Aug. 27, 2004, p.C7
*Long Beach Press-Telegram,* Dec. 3, 2003
*Los Angeles Magazine,* June 1, 2004, p.48
*Los Angeles Times,* Oct. 16, 1994, p.25; Sep. 25, 1997, p.10
*New York Times,* Aug. 25, 2004, p.D5
*Oakland Tribune,* Aug. 16, 2004
*San Francisco Chronicle,* May 7, 2003, p.C2
*USA Today,* June 23, 2004, p.C7; Mar. 29, 2005, p.C4

### Online Articles

http://www.stanfordalumni.org
    (*Stanford Magazine,* "Seniors Enter International Waters,"
    July-Aug. 2003)

## ADDRESS

Brenda Villa
U.S. National Women's Water Polo Team
11360 Valley Forge
Los Alamitos, CA 90720

## WORLD WIDE WEB SITES

http://gostanford.collegesports.com
http://www.usawaterpolo.org

# Photo and Illustration Credits

Carol Bellamy/Photos: U.N. Photo/Stephenie Hollyman (p. 9); Nancy R. Schiff/Hulton Archive/Getty Images (p. 12); Shah Marai/AFP/Getty Images (p. 14); AP Images (p. 16).

Miri Ben-Ari/Photos: Adam Weiss/copyright © 2003 Universal Music Group (p. 19); Frank Micelotta/Getty Images (p. 22). CD cover: THE HIP-HOP VIOLINIST copyright © 2003 Universal Music Group.

Dale Chihuly/Photos: Dale Chihuly photo/Russell Johnson (p. 28); Chihuly and team in hotshop, Seattle, Wash. photo/Russell Johnson (p. 32); *Shell Pink Basket Set with Oxblood Wraps*, 1995, 9 × 22 × 22″, photo/Dick Busher (p. 35); *White Seaform with Black Lip Wraps*, 1990, 14 × 25 × 19″, photo/Teresa N. Rishel (p. 37); *Macchia Forest*, 2002 photo/Teresa N. Rishel (p. 39); *Gilded Silver and Aquamarine Chandelier*, 2000, 96 × 102″, photo/Jan Cook. Front cover: *Cerise Orange Basket Set with Onyx Lip Wraps*, 1997, 15 × 15 × 15″. Photo: Scott M. Leen.

Dakota Fanning/Photos: Susy Wood/Paramount Pictures (p. 44); Lorey Sebastian/copyright © 2001 New Line Cinema (p. 47); Melinda Sue Gordon/copyright © 2003 Universal Studios and DreamWorks LLC (p. 49, top); copyright © 2003 Metro-Goldwyn-Mayer Pictures, Inc. (p. 49, middle); Joe Lederer/TM & copyright © DreamWorks LLC (p. 49, bottom).

Russel Honoré/Photos: AP Images (p. 54); Justin Sullivan/Getty Images (p. 57); NOAA/Getty Images P. 58); Paul J. Richards/AFP/Getty Images (p. 60); Nicholas Kamm/AFP/Getty Images (p. 63). Front cover: AP Images.

Steve Nash/Photos: Jeff Gross/Getty Images (p. 66); Otto Greule, Jr./Getty Images (p. 68); AP Images (pp. 71, 73, 78); Robert Galbraith/Reuters/Landov (p. 75).

Lil' Romeo/Photos: Nickelodeon/David Ellingsen (p. 81, 87); Tim Alexander/copyright © 2003 Universal Music Group (p. 83); Mike Heffner/Getty Images (p. 90). CD cover: LIL' ROMEO (p) & copyright © 2001 Soulja Music Entertainment/Priority Records LLC.

Adam Sandler/Photos: Vera Anderson/WireImage.com (p. 93); NBC Universal photo (p. 96); Kimberly Wright/New Line Cinema (p. 103, top); Joseph Lederer/copyright © 1996 Universal City Studios, Inc. (p. 103, middle); Myles Aronowitz/copyright © 1999 Columbia Pictures Industries, Inc. (p. 103, bottom); Darren Michaels/copyright © 2004 Columbia Pictures Industries, Inc. (p. 106); TM & copyright © 2005 by Paramount Pictures (p. 109). DVD cover: BILLY MADISON copyright © 1995 Universal Studios. Front cover: Tracy Bennett/Paramount Pictures.

Jon Stewart/Photos: Norman Jean Roy/Comedy Central (p. 113); Evan Agnosti/Getty Images (p. 115); Todd Pitt/Getty Images (p. 117); Al Levine/Comedy Central (p. 119). Cover: AMERICA (THE BOOK): A CITIZEN'S GUIDE TO DEMOCRACY INACTION (Warner Books, 2004). Jacket design by Pentagram. Jacket photograph by Andrew Eccles.

Joss Stone/Photos: Newscom.com (p. 126); copyright © Camera Press/ Josh Rothstein/Retna (p. 129); Christopher Furlong/Getty Images (p. 130). CD cover: MIND, BODY & SOUL (p) & copyright © 2004 EMI Music North America. Front cover: AP Images.

Brenda Villa/Photos: Daniel Hankin/USA Water Polo (p. 135); Christophe Simon/AFP/Getty Images (p. 139); David Gonzales/Stanford Athletics (p. 140); Daniel Berehulak/Getty Images (p. 142).

# Cumulative Names Index

This cumulative index includes the names of all individuals profiled in *Biography Today* since the debut of the series in 1992.

For cumulative general, places of birth, and birthday indexes, please see biographytoday.com.

For cumulative general, places of birth, and birthday indexes, please see biographytoday.com.

For cumulative general, places of birth, and birthday indexes, please see biographytoday.com.

For cumulative general, places of birth, and birthday indexes, please see biographytoday.com.

For cumulative general, places of birth, and birthday indexes, please see biographytoday.com.

For cumulative general, places of birth, and birthday indexes, please see biographytoday.com.

# Biography Today

## General Series

**For ages 9 and above**

*iography Today* **General Series** includes a unique combination of current biographical profiles that teachers and librarians — and the readers themselves — tell us are most appealing. The **General Series** is available as a 3-issue subscription; hardcover annual cumulation; or subscription plus cumulation.

Within the **General Series**, your readers will find a variety of sketches about:

- Authors
- Musicians
- Political leaders
- Sports figures
- Movie actresses & actors
- Cartoonists
- Scientists
- Astronauts
- TV personalities
- and the movers & shakers in many other fields!

"*Biography Today* will be useful in elementary and middle school libraries and in public library children's collections where there is a need for biographies of current personalities. High schools serving reluctant readers may also want to consider a subscription."
— *Booklist,* American Library Association

"Highly recommended for the young adult audience. Readers will delight in the accessible, energetic, tell-all style; teachers, librarians, and parents will welcome the clever format [and] intelligent and informative text. It should prove especially useful in motivating 'reluctant' readers or literate nonreaders."
— *MultiCultural Review*

"Written in a friendly, almost chatty tone, the profiles offer quick, objective information. While coverage of current figures makes *Biography Today* a useful reference tool, an appealing format and wide scope make it a fun resource to browse." — *School Library Journal*

"The best source for current information at a level kids can understand."
— Kelly Bryant, School Librarian, Carlton, OR

"Easy for kids to read. We love it! Don't want to be without it."
— Lynn McWhirter, School Librarian, Rockford, IL

### ONE-YEAR SUBSCRIPTION
- 3 softcover issues, 6" x 9"
- Published in January, April, and September
- 1-year subscription, list price $62. **School and library price $60**
- 150 pages per issue
- 10 profiles per issue
- Contact sources for additional information
- Cumulative Names Index

### HARDBOUND ANNUAL CUMULATION
- Sturdy 6" x 9" hardbound volume
- Published in December
- List price $69. **School and library price $62 per volume**
- 450 pages per volume
- 30 profiles — includes all profiles found in softcover issues for that calendar year
- Cumulative General Index

### SUBSCRIPTION AND CUMULATION COMBINATION
- $99 for 3 softcover issues plus the hardbound volume

**For Cumulative General, Places of Birth, and Birthday Indexes, please see www.biographytoday.com.**

# Biography Today

## Subject Series

**For ages 9 and above**

### Expands and complements the General Series and targets specific subject areas ...

Our readers asked for it! They wanted more biographies, and the *Biography Today* **Subject Series** is our response to that demand. Now your readers can choose their special areas of interest and go on to read about their favorites in those fields. The following specific volumes are included in the *Biography Today* **Subject Series**:

- **Authors**
- **Business Leaders**
- **Performing Artists**
- **Scientists & Inventors**
- **Sports**

### FEATURES AND FORMAT

- Sturdy 6" x 9" hardbound volumes
- Individual volumes, list price $44 each. **School and library price $39 each**
- 200 pages per volume
- 10 profiles per volume — targets individuals within a specific subject area
- Contact sources for additional information
- Cumulative General Index

**For Cumulative General, Places of Birth, and Birthday Indexes, please see www.biographytoday.com.**

**NOTE:** There is *no duplication of entries* between the **General Series** of *Biography Today* and the **Subject Series**.

### AUTHORS

"A useful tool for children's assignment needs." — *School Library Journal*

"The prose is workmanlike: report writers will find enough detail to begin sound investigations, and browsers are likely to find someone of interest." — *School Library Journal*

### SCIENTISTS & INVENTORS

"The articles are readable, attractively laid out, and touch on important points that will suit assignment needs. Browsers will note the clear writing and interesting details." — *School Library Journal*

"The book is excellent for demonstrating that scientists are real people with widely diverse backgrounds and personal interests. The biographies are fascinating to read." — *The Science Teacher*

### SPORTS

"This series should become a standard resource in libraries that serve intermediate students." — *School Library Journal*